EXEGETICAL M

A Student's Handbook

OTTO KAISER
and
WERNER GEORG KÜMMEL

Translated, with an Introduction, by
E. V. N. GOETCHIUS

THE SEABURY PRESS · NEW YORK

Copyright © 1963 by Chr. Kaiser Verlag, München
Translation copyright © 1967 by E. V. N. Goetchius
Library of Congress Catalog Card Number: 67-15734
Design by Nancy Dale
569-667-H-3.5
Printed in the United States of America

CONTENTS

INTRODUCTION

❖ ❖ ❖

by the Translator

The following essays, by Professors Kaiser and Küm-mel, were written at the request of the Association of German Evangelical Theological Students. In them the authors seek to provide such guidance as will enable beginning students to pursue exegetical studies with understanding and enjoyment.

It is unfortunately possible for students—in any field of study and at any level—to plod along without ever learning to pursue their studies with real understanding and without ever knowing the satisfaction such understanding can bring; it is especially unfortunate that this should be true in the field of biblical exegesis, for here the student has every right to expect to gain insight into the original documents and seminal concepts of Christianity, which should be a source of great satisfaction for every student of the history of ideas, and especially for a Christian student. But, alas, all too frequently biblical exegesis is made to appear not as a field in which scientific inquiries are pursued by orderly methods, but as a vale of mystery where dwell the "Higher Critics"—a Babel of commentators constantly disagreeing with one another. This happens especially when professors rely exclusively on lectures, as they sometimes feel pressed to do, in order to present a large body of material in a limited time. It is obvious, of course, that lectures on biblical exegesis can, at worst, degenerate into a mere cataloguing of conflicting opinions, submerging the student in a welter of names and facts and reducing him to a note-taking automaton, condemned to memorizing the "assured results" of other people's work and effectively barred from coming to grips with exegetical problems for himself. In these circumstances it is no wonder that students lose interest and close their commentaries—and sometimes their Bibles as well—when they leave seminary. However, even under optimum conditions, even with an inspired lecturer, the student at a lecture is cast in a passive role: he is only an auditor, a nonparticipant in the business at hand. Biblical exegesis is not a spectator sport, and lectures are not enough.

Real understanding, and concomitant enjoyment, in any kind of study comes as the result of creative and independent thinking, and the ability of students to think independently and creatively can be most effectually developed by encouraging them to explore problems in their own way. It is obvious that this "discovery approach," as it is called,[1] has limitations. If given no assistance whatever, even the best students will flounder, and most students will abandon the whole enterprise in frustration. To ensure a reasonable rate of advancement, then, as well as to maintain interest, independent study must be supplemented by classroom discussion, in which the teacher, in dialogue with the class, guides the students through the analysis of problems. The amount of guidance necessary will, of course, vary with circumstances; at the very least the teacher will assist students in the identification and statement of exegetical problems and will direct them to the resources available for the solution of these problems. For a beginning, the teacher can hardly do better than to direct his students

[1] Cf. *Goals for School Mathematics: The Report of the Cambridge Conference on School Mathematics* (Boston: Houghton Mifflin, 1963).

to the essays in this book. A student who reads these essays carefully and works through the illustrative problems by himself will be well prepared to work out similar problems alone or with little guidance, and then to move on with his teacher—intelligently rather than blindly—to more complicated questions.

Finally, a student who has learned to work in this way can proceed naturally and confidently to apply the procedures he has learned to other fields of study in which they are appropriate or to which they can be adapted, for there is nothing specifically biblical, or even sacred, about the approach we have been discussing. Indeed, there is really no substitute for this kind of work in exegetical study, just as there is no substitute for laboratory work in the study of the natural sciences. A student who learns to work in this way—both independently and in creative dialogue with his teachers and fellow students—will find his ability and his interest, and consequently his enjoyment, increasing, and though he may not "cover all the material" in his seminary years, he will not soon forget what he has learned, and he will be able and interested to continue his studies after his graduation, to the obvious enrichment of his ministry.

The original German edition included a third essay by Gottfried Adam, a student at the University of Marburg, dealing with the technical side of studying: note-taking, preparation of reports and papers, use of the library, and so on. This has been omitted since much of it is oriented toward the special circumstances of a German university, and much also is already available elsewhere.

Some of the following may be found helpful: William H. Armstrong, *Study Is Hard Work* (New York: Harper, 1956); Adrian A. Paradis, *The Research Handbook* (New York: Funk and Wagnalls, 1966); Kathleen Dugdale, *A Manual on Writing Research* and *A Manual of Form for*

Theses and Term Reports (both published by: Blooming-ton, Ind.: University of Indiana Press, 1962); B. Metzger, *A Guide to the Preparation of a Thesis* (Princeton, N.J.: Princeton Theological Seminary, 1961); Edward D. Seeber, *A Style Manual for Students* (University of Indiana Press, 1966); Lewis Jordan (ed.), *The New York Times Style Book* (New York: McGraw-Hill, 1962); *A Manual of Style* (11th ed.; Chicago: University of Chicago Press, 1947); Jacques Barzun and Henry F. Graff, *The Modern Researcher* (New York: Harcourt, Brace & World, 1957; Harbinger Books, 1962).

Otto Kaiser

✤ ✤ ✤

OLD TESTAMENT EXEGESIS

I. Exegesis and Proclamation

We shall take it for granted that in the final analysis all theological endeavor serves as a preparation for the proclamation of the gospel, by means of which God himself intends to bring about living faith in Jesus Christ as Lord of the world and as Lord of His Church (Augustine, *Confessions,* §5). The Church necessarily expresses its faith in a creed with which it confronts the individual Christian. Thereby it offers a normative proclamation and a standard for the faith of the individual. But the Church as a whole, like the proclamation which takes place in its midst and like the faith of the individual Christian, is referred back to the Holy Scripture as the source and norm of faith. In ever-renewed hearing of the testimony of Scripture, the creed of the Church will be examined, interpreted, and, if need be, modified; in ever-renewed hearing of the testimony of Scripture, the proclamation of the gospel will be prepared; in ever-renewed hearing of the testimony of Scripture, the faith of the individual will be challenged, purified, strengthened, and confirmed.[1] Since the Holy Scriptures of the Old and New Testaments are primarily a historical record of God's saving activity on behalf of men that belongs to the past, the re-presentation of this record forms the basis of all creedal statements, all proclamation, and all faith in the Church. In the service of this re-presentation, all theological endeavor is performed within the various theological disciplines and especially, in accordance with what has just been said, in the exegesis of the Old and New Testaments.

As an act of human understanding, exegesis cannot be without presuppositions. Every exegete, as a human being who is affected by existential questions, brings with him definite preconceptions and prejudices.[2] It is decisive for personal faith and for the proclamation which should issue from it that the encounter with and analysis of the testimony of the Scripture as a whole as well as the testimony of each individual book or section of Scripture should and must result in involving the exegete's own understanding of himself as this has been challenged by the testimony of Scripture. But in order that the testimony of Scripture may be truly heard and in order that a real encounter with this testimony may follow upon this hearing, it is essential to proceed without bias, strange though this may sound at first and, in the last analysis, limited though this requirement must be. The interpreter must first be prepared to suspend the dogmatic convictions of the Church, the traditional views of scholarship, and even his own understanding of the faith in order to listen with true objectivity to the text which lies before him.[3] The much misunderstood saying, that it is the task of the interpreter to understand a writer better than he understood himself, is applicable here only in the restricted sense that the exegete is obliged "to explain the background out of which the expression concerned has arisen."[4] Understood in this way, this requirement is perfectly consistent with that of an unbiased, impartial exegesis —that is, since Scripture deals with matters pertaining to the past, of historical critical exegesis. The knowledge of the methods of such exegesis and the ability to use these methods are therefore indispensable both for scholarly study of Holy Scripture and for sermon preparation. The neglect of this kind of exegesis leads unavoidably to eccentricity in theology and to the impoverishment of preaching and, hence, even to a betrayal of the Church to heretics[5] and to compromising the faith.

In the framework of a basic introduction to the methods of historical critical exegesis of Old Testament texts it cannot be our task to pursue either the hermeneutical problem in general or the problems involved in a Christian understanding of the Old Testament in particular.[6] For the student the first question—quite apart from the question of what definite confessional tradition he has grown up in or that of whether or not he takes up his theological work of his own free choice—is how to become acquainted with the methods of procedure that are of crucial importance in exegesis and with the scholarly resources that are at his disposal for pursuing these. In order not to burden this introduction from the beginning with a systematic prior judgment, we will therefore consciously abstain from a detailed discussion of existential interpretation.

II. Text of the Old Testament— Textual Criticism

A reliable, critically edited text in the original language forms the general basis of every scholarly pursuit connected with the Old Testament and, consequently, is the basis for our exegetical work. We have this in the form of the *Biblia Hebraica,* edited by Rudolf Kittel; since the third edition, which was completed in 1937, this has been based on the oldest completely preserved manuscript of the Hebrew Bible, the Codex Leningradensis, which dates from the year A.D. 1008. Along with this one should make use of a translation which satisfies scholarly requirements, such as we have in the American Standard Version (1901),[7] The

Holy Bible: A New Translation by James Moffatt (1926), The Bible: An American Translation (1931),[8] The Revised Standard Version (1952),[9] and more recent translations.[10] Here may also be mentioned *The Apocrypha and Pseudepigrapha of the Old Testament in English,* edited by R. H. Charles.[11]

First of all we try to get a preliminary feeling for the text to be interpreted by reading it aloud several times, and then we make a rough translation which will serve as the basis for further work. By reading the text aloud we should become so familiar with it that any interpretation we may afterward give will really be an interpretation of the text and not an interpretation of our rough translation or of some other version. We place the lexicon and grammar, which are our primary aids, within easy reach.[12]

The next step is the recovery of the text, or *textual criticism*. For from the very nature of the biblical manuscript tradition, which lasted for hundreds and even thousands of years, with all the conscious alterations and unconscious distortions connected with it, it follows that the text to be explained must first be established. In the ideal case of a scientific edition of the text—such as the third edition of the *Biblia Hebraica* represents, approximately, for its time—one will take into account all the available witnesses to the text in the original language and in the translations made in the period of manuscript diffusion, using the oldest complete manuscript in the original language as a basis, directly or indirectly; however, the student will usually have to be—but also *can* be—content to use appropriate editions of the Greek and Latin Bibles, the Septuagint and the Vulgate[13] and, if occasion demands, also the Samaritan Pentateuch[14] and the scrolls and fragments discovered in the desert of Judea.[15] Methodologically reliable work in textual criticism presupposes a knowledge of the history of the Hebrew text and its translations, as this is set forth in the introductions to the Old Testament[16] and other specialized works.[17] A survey of the history of the text, the available editions, and detailed instruction in textual criticism are given especially by E. Würthwein, *The Text of the Old Testament*,[18] and M. Noth, *The Old Testament World*.[19] Both books belong in the hands of every student.

Textual criticism proceeds in three steps: the collection and arrangement of the variants, the examination of the variants and, finally, the determination of the correct reading (or the most likely reading). In the first step the variant readings found in the manuscript tradition are arranged in the order in which they arose in the history of the text.[20] Here it is necessary to note only such variants as are neither intentional alterations nor later assimilations to the Masoretic text. In the same way mechanical scribal errors are separated out at this step. Next the traditional text is examined on the basis of linguistic evidence and the evidence of the subject matter. Here the Masoretic text, as it appears in the *Biblia Hebraica,* deserves most careful attention. If considerations appear against it, the range of meaning of doubtful words is first of all to be investigated lexically, and then the linguistic usage is to be examined with the help of a Hebrew concordance.[21] A similar procedure should be followed in regard to the Greek variants. In determining the range of meaning for a Greek word,[22] the investigation of the Hebrew equivalents for it may be a factor. Here the work of E. Hatch and H. A. Redpath, *A Concordance to the Septuagint and the Other Greek Versions of the Old Testament,* last reprinted in Graz in 1954, affords indispensable aid; for here, after the Greek word, the actual Hebrew equivalents are listed, and the Hebrew equivalent in each separate passage is indicated. Before it is established that a Hebrew phrase cannot be rendered in

Greek, the parallels must be examined, and these must be looked up in the Hebrew concordance.

As befits a beginner, one will challenge the text on the basis of metrical and form-critical considerations in the course of a metrical investigation just as in literary criticism, which is sometimes referred to as "higher" criticism in contradistinction to "lower" or textual criticism. However, a certain amount of overlapping of the steps of exegesis cannot ordinarily be avoided in the examination of the subject matter; there may always be occasion for this, if a single word or expression does not fit well in the context of the Old Testament world. It will probably already be clear at this point that the individual steps of exegesis must first be taken up in a definite order, but that later on, when writing down one's findings, the whole must be kept in view and the interrelationship of the parts clearly shown, i.e., that the arrangement and order of the methodological steps must proceed on each occasion in accordance with the particular task. In determining the value of witnesses to the text one will always give preference to the Masoretic text, unless it is "impossible on grounds of language or context."[23] Only if the Masoretic text is untenable are the variant readings of the other textual witnesses to be examined. The Hebrew text is always to be corrected in accordance with these if sufficient grounds for their originality can be produced. Only when none of the traditional variants has any claim to originality is it admissible to emend a corrupt passage by means of a conjecture. Chiefly in the books from Joshua to Kings do the Hebrew and Greek texts differ widely. Before a decision is made here in a particular case, the special nature of the particular tradition is to be pursued through several chapters. In this way a short text in the Septuagint that at first seems attractive may very soon be shown to be secondary.

III. Analysis of the Meter

If we are dealing with a metrical text, the meter involved must be examined in connection with the textual
criticism. Here it will be borne in mind from the start that
a primary difficulty of every metrical construction is that
the system of accentuation now lying before us in the Masoretic text was not fixed until many centuries after the written
text itself. A second decisive difficulty is that up to now no
unanimous agreement has been reached among investigators
as to what metrical system underlies Hebrew poetry. Even
if one is persuaded that the meter is accentual—rather than
a quantitative one, which depends for its effect on various
combinations of long and short syllables—one must still
determine whether it is an alternating meter, with each
accented syllable followed by an unaccented one, or whether
it is anapaestic, with two unaccented syllables followed by
a single accented one. It may be said, however, that up to
now most scholars incline to the opinion that Hebrew meter
was accentual and anapaestic.[24] In view of all the questions
which are still in dispute, one should introduce metrical
considerations into one's argument only if some objective
points can be convincingly made. The beginner is especially
urged to exercise the greatest restraint here.

IV. Literary Criticism

Since an understanding of authorship in the modern
sense is lacking in the Old Testament period, we must
reckon with the fact that the individual books do not repre-
sent unified literary compositions. They are, rather, collections and reworkings of earlier traditions, some of which
were oral in nature but others of which were already independent documentary sources or small independent units,

which may or may not have been previously arranged and worked over. Needless to say, the standpoints from which these "books" or collections were edited varied greatly. This history of the text determines the task of literary criticism, the goal of which is to separate the original content of a book, of a source document, or of an individual tradition from later accretions and thereby to pave the way for a historical evaluation of the text.

The work of literary criticism begins with the examination of the structure or internal arrangement of a portion of the text. It leads at once to an understanding of the whole text and is, therefore, to be undertaken with great care. It is convenient to proceed in three steps: first, each portion of the text is classified according to the point of view—dramatic or functional—from which it has been composed; there may, of course, be some overlapping in these classifications. At this stage a basic knowledge of the various prose and poetic genres which are to be found in the Old Testament is already necessary.[25] Thus it is clear that the analysis is of decisive importance not only for literary criticism, but also for the identification of genres and for the total understanding of the text. In a second step the train of thought expressed in the text is to be traced from sentence to sentence and examined for possible inconsistencies. By working through the text repeatedly in this way, doublets, secondary glosses, alternations between poetry and prose, stylistic deviations, omissions, shifts in thought and direct contradictions are brought to light, if any are present. On the basis of this and the metrical analysis which has, if necessary, been done previously, the real work of literary criticism follows. First, the obvious glosses are eliminated.

Next, the main strands of the narrative or other unity

which underlies the text are worked out, and then the subordinate sources or stages in the process of revision are established. For the evaluation of the results obtained it is necessary to have some knowledge of the results obtained by literary-critical research up to the present and an acquaintance with the competing hypotheses that have been based upon it. This may be gained with the help of the introductions[26] or the relevant monographs and commentaries. It is hardly necessary to emphasize that the examination of the linguistic usage of the source documents, narrative strata, prophetic oracles and the like must be made with great care, so that, in the case of a limited piece of research, the results of other investigators must be considered.[27] In working with linguistic statistics, using the concordance with special analytical surveys, it is essential to bear in mind that different subjects can require different vocabularies. Nevertheless, it is possible to give definite answers to many problems if the history of single words or whole phrases is investigated with sufficient thoroughness.

In addition to the Hebrew concordance, the introductions, relevant monographs, and commentaries will again be found useful. However, the student should make it a rule for himself here as in all other exegetical procedures, to take up the secondary literature only if he has, on the basis of his own researches, already arrived at a definite, even if necessarily provisional, result. If he does not observe this rule he will fall into a dependence on the literature which can very quickly rob his work of all scientific value and which, moreover, will deprive him of all joy in his work. Furthermore, he can judge the weight of the points of view set forth in the different individual works, since he can compare several works with each other. Here we do not mean to endorse some kind of numerical procedure that is inappropriate within this science, but merely to indicate how the beginner can recognize whether he is dealing with one hypothesis among many or whether he has to do with an opinion which is already generally accepted by scholars. It goes without saying, of course, that even the latter can always be disproved by clear and concise arguments. In a written scholarly paper the beginner should, if the state of the question requires no more, content himself with giving a clear presentation of the literary critical findings, to set forth the interpretations of his findings which have already been accepted in the scholarly tradition and, at most, to point out as such the one interpretation which appears to him to fit the findings in question most adequately.

A hint of the broader narrative contexts and also of an original or actual independence of the textual unit under consideration may be obtained from an examination of the manner in which the text is joined to the material that precedes it and to that which follows it. Here it is not always possible to limit oneself to a consideration of the chapters immediately preceding or following, since sections which were originally closely connected may very probably have been separated from each other by redactional work. If clear internal and possibly also form-critical evidence points to the independence of the unit, the examination of the "joints" at its beginning and end at least reveals preliminary standpoints for the understanding of the composition of the book or the method followed by the author or editor in his work. In the subsequent steps of exegesis the results of the literary criticism are to be taken into account in such a way that the text under consideration is explained from one stage of development to another. It should be clear, consequently, that literary criticism is no more an end in itself than is textual criticism, but is an essential key to the understanding of the text.

V. Form Criticism and Tradition Criticism[27a]

When the boundaries of the prose or poetic unit have
been marked off, the next task is the determination of the
genre, which in turn allows us to reason back to the original
Sitz im Leben.[28] We always speak of a genre if a definite
form is united with a definite content and if both possess a
fixed point of reference, a definite *Sitz im Leben*. Let us
turn here to Hermann Gunkel, the father of research into
Old Testament genres:

The literary products of primitive times and places are
distinguished from those of more civilized peoples in that they
are not, like the latter, imaginable almost only on paper, but
arise out of the actual life of human beings and have their Sitz
im Leben in it: women sing the triumphant psalm of victory as
they go out to meet the returning victorious army; or the trem-
bling dirge is wailed over the bier of the dead, perhaps by pro-
fessional mourners; or the prophet lets his voice thunder forth
before the assembled community, it may be in the forecourt of
the sanctuary. In such examples, which could be greatly multi-
plied, one sees . . . *that the genres of a primitive literature have
to be distinguished according to the different occasions of life*.[29]

Since the individuality of the narrator or poet plays a
much more restricted role at that time than it does among
modern peoples, the poetical genres reveal their identity
more particularly by a distinctive "form language" and,
further, by "a common treasury of ideas and moods." Fairy
tale, saga, sermon, and hymn may still be known as such
today by a distinctive style and also by a distinctive vocabulary and range of ideas, even if only a portion of them
comes to our hearing or sight. We must, however, be conscious, during the process of analysis, of the fact that in the
course of development, and more particularly in the course

of the rise of a literature properly so called, a mixture of genres took place, so that we must guard against a "puristic" procedure.

If a genre is characterized by the union of form and content, it is clear that stylistic analysis must have a place in the process of genre analysis. In spite of much preparatory spade work—done, for the most part, by Gunkel, Eissfeldt, Alt, Hölscher, and Westermann[30]—it must be admitted that the stylistic analysis of the Old Testament is still in its infancy. The object of stylistic analysis is to understand "what language can do and how it does it."[31] Stylistic analysis presupposes an attention to the linguistic forms, the wording, the kinds of words used, the rhetorical figures, the word order, the syntactic forms, the types of sentences, and the modes and forms of expression, but it is not exhausted in such formal observations. Fundamentally, it requires an intuitive process of discovery, and should, therefore, proceed from repeated and careful reading— which should also be reading *aloud*—in the course of which definite peculiarities of style will, as it were, obtrude themselves upon our attention. How stylistic analysis can provide an essential contribution to the understanding of an author's intention is shown by E. Auerbach in *Mimesis: the Representation of Reality in Western Literature*,[32] a work which can be recommended to both beginners and advanced students. Here, in the example of the account of Isaac's sacrifice in Genesis, chapter 22, it is shown how the biblical narratives intend no "sensory magic" and therefore describe the physical world only so far as is necessary, "because the moral, religious, and psychological phenomena which are their sole concern are made concrete in the sensible matter of life."[33] God's claim to lordship over men, which is made in the Scriptures, lays hold upon them in their everyday affairs and thus prevents the separation of the sublime and the ordinary. On the basis of this claim we may understand the stylistic peculiarities, which Auerbach describes as the emphasizing of some details and the de-emphasizing of others, as "roughness, suggestive effect of the unexpressed, allusiveness, ambiguity, starkness of detail, universality of claim, concept of historical development, deepening of the nature of the problematical."[34] In the stylistic analysis of Hebrew poetry, it is essential to note the explanations in the introductions dealing with the various types of parallelism (*parallelismus membrorum*).

Within the poetic categories may be recognized the motifs, the determinative formal elements such as, e.g., the introduction to the "hymn or descriptive eulogy," with its summons to praise; the main section, which sets out the reasons for this; and the conclusion, which is frequently similar in content and form to the introduction. Since Israelite poetry was in its turn an inheritor of ancient oriental culture, a preliminary survey of the cultural and religious history of the surrounding world is basic to the investigation of its categories, as is similarly the case with the study of Old Testament legal maxims.[35] One should proceed with special circumspection in determining the categories of prophetic texts, since the prophets made use not only of the prophetic categories properly so called, i.e., the "threat or announcement of judgment," the "invective or accusation," the "promise," and the "warning," but also of other profane and cultic categories. The "accusation" is almost always joined to an "announcement of judgment" to form a "substantiated announcement of judgment"; and the "warning" is similarly joined to an "announcement of judgment [or of salvation]" to form a "conditional announcement of judgment [or conditional promise]." If we disregard prayers in the narrow sense, the categories employed by the prophets may always be classified as one or another of the forms of discourse mentioned above as properly prophetic.[36] The expositor must therefore occasionally give an account of the function of an element of discourse within the larger unit of discourse under consideration. It is still in dispute whether the prophets left behind them only short discourses or whether they also left longer ones; this question can hardly be decided in general, but only in particular cases. Apart from historiography, which reached its high point—never again attained in Israelite literature—in the "Story of the Succession to the Throne of David" in 2 Samuel, chapters 7-20 and 1 Kings, chapters 1-2, we shall, when dealing with prose categories, have to distinguish first of all between the heroic sagas and the etiological sagas. The latter take their name from the fact that they attempt to answer questions about the *aitia* or cause of existing facts, customs, place names, and so forth. In determining the category and the original *Sitz im Leben* the expositor will disregard the fact that an individual story has been imbedded in a larger context, for previous research has been able to show indisputably that individual stories arose in the stage of oral tradition and led their own life entirely until they grew together, in a complicated process, to the saga cycles we now possess.[37]

While the real purpose and, therefore, at the same time, the *Sitz im Leben* are relatively easy to establish for the poetic and prophetic categories, greater insight is often necessary to distinguish the narrative categories. As one approaches this task one will have to ask oneself occasionally what class of people could have had special interest in what is being reported, and what institution or group of persons could benefit from it. Here a possible localization of the story gives a first indication of the homeland of the tradition.

Tradition criticism arises quite independently out of

form criticism or genre criticism: for poetic texts it is needed for the investigation of the store of formal language commonly used in a genre for the expression of particular thoughts and moods, and for prophetic texts it is needed for similar reasons. It is especially necessary since portions of text which have undergone extensive editorial reworking contain a whole compendium of Israelite literary and religious history. By tracing back the motifs that have been taken over by the prophets from the fundamental traditions preserved in the cultus, we are able to open up a view into the history of the cultus as far as the dim prehistory of Israel. By investigating the secondary additions and the additions that are, perhaps, literary and editorial in the strict sense, we may be led as far as the time of the Maccabees. Legislative texts frequently point back beyond themselves in the same way; some, being formulated as statements of absolute truth, raise the question of their *Sitz im Leben* in the worship of Israel; others, casuistically formulated, refer back to the Israelite legal community and the administration of justice "in the gate"; and, at the same time, they also point back to their roots in the Canaanite province of ancient oriental legal culture.[38] Finally, the problem of how the original individual units came to be in their present context must be considered. How did the individual saga find its way into the saga cycle and then into a source document? How did the source document come to be combined with others to form the present book or books? How does it happen that a common design may be recognized in different source documents? All of these questions require a tradition-critical answer.[39] It should be immediately obvious that the pattern emerging in this way depends upon insights drawn from the history of religion as well as from literary criticism; in the same way, it is apparent that this work reveals new insights which are important chiefly for the understanding of the prehistory and early history of Israel. Every evaluation of an Old Testament text for the reconstruction of the history of Israel remains amateurish unless the text is examined beforehand from the standpoints of literary criticism, form criticism, and tradition criticism. The mere accumulation of a vast number of parallels from the history of religion and culture cannot release one from the historian's obligation to subject his sources to criticism in the senses just mentioned.[40]

What was true for the results obtained by literary criticism with regard to the further work of form criticism and tradition criticism is now true for form criticism and tradition criticism with regard to the later steps of exegesis: the interpreter has to keep them constantly in mind when formulating further explanations, especially when he is engaged in context exegesis, i.e., the interpretation of a text in relationship to its context. In this way he is restrained from asking improper questions of his text and thereby shortcircuiting his exegesis by psychologizing, historicizing, or romanticizing it in some other way.

VI. Subject Exegesis, Concept Exegesis, and Context Exegesis

Exegesis in the narrower sense deals with the subject matter of the text, with the concepts involved, and with the context to which the text belongs. Insofar as these aspects of exegesis may be considered separately, it is convenient to speak of them as subject exegesis (*Sachexegese*), concept exegesis (*Begriffsexegese*), and context exegesis (*Zusammenhangsexegese*). In subject exegesis, which may appropriately be dealt with first, all persons, institutions, and facts of various kinds (e.g., indications of place, architecture, furniture, utensils, and the like) which are mentioned in the text are noted and identified. Here the historical situation presupposed by the text is explained, if need be in the ✓ form of an excursus, if direct clues to it are found in the text. In this work also, the beginner should again beware of having the results suggested immediately by a commentary or reference book. Instead he will begin again with the lexicon and, if need be, investigate other occurrences of related matters in the Old Testament with the help of a concordance; thus he will endeavor to obtain a picture of the situation which, at least at first, is independently arrived at. For the persons mentioned he will next, with the help of Köhler's *Lexicon* and the special literature referred to there or with the help of a Bible dictionary,[41] determine the derivation of the names and their significance, and he will look up the historical connections—in the case of Israelite names, in a history of Israel; in the case of non-Israelite names, in a history of the Near East in antiquity.[42]

The identification of biblical place names presents a special problem; first, the location of many places is still disputed, and second, the student frequently finds himself in difficulty if he looks into an atlas, since besides the biblical names it may also give the modern Arabic or Israeli names. Moreover, since he does not always have time to follow up the diverging lines of investigation which suggest themselves in the course of a comprehensive exegetical task, he will, if nothing decisive depends on the correctness of the identification, rely primarily on the information of a Bible dictionary, of Köhler's *Lexicon,* or of the list of place names appended by M. Noth to his commentary on Joshua (*HAT* 7, Tübingen 1953², pp. 142-151).[43] It should go without saying that places looked up in this way should also be identified on a map.[44]

For information about such facts as architecture, utensils, and furniture, one will turn first to the *Biblisches Lexikon* of K. Galling[45] and afterward to the Bible dictionaries mentioned in note 41, above. For complete under-

standing of the statements made there, a certain basic
acquaintance with archeological methods and results is prerequisite; an adequate discussion of these may be found in
M. Noth's *Old Testament World*,[46] in the *Primer of Old
Testament Archeology* by H. J. Franken and C. A. Franken-
Battershill,[47] and elsewhere.[48] A description of the concrete
aspects of life in Old Testament times is given by F. Nöt-
scher in his *Biblische Altertumskunde*[49] as well as by M.
Noth in his *Old Testament World;*[50] in the latter work only
the contribution of archeology is taken into account. G.
Dalman's *Arbeit und Sitte in Palästina* (I-VII, Gütersloh,
1928-42) will be found indispensable again and again. For
the gathering of material about Old Testament institutions
the work of R. de Vaux, *Ancient Israel: Its Life and Institutions*,[51] is also useful. The first part deals with the organi-
zation of the state and the family, while in the second the
details of the military and cultic establishments are described. In collecting material on all matters connected with
religion one can often employ the standard works on Old
Testament theology, though these are not designed primarily
as reference books.[52] When preparing a written account of
the exegesis of a text from the point of view of its subject
matter—as well as, later on, of the corresponding concept
exegesis—one should include only what is immediately
necessary for the understanding of the text and its background. If a more extensive explanation of one's findings is
necessary, or if a decision must be made between conflicting
points of view, these will most appropriately be dealt with
in excursuses.

Concept exegesis, which follows next, involves the exact understanding of the content of the theological and
other leading ideas. Practically speaking, this task is also
approached with the help of the dictionary and the Hebrew
concordance. As in the case of the preceding steps of
exegesis, the secondary literature is used only after the inter-

preter has formed an opinion of his own, however provisional. Thus, in the first place, parallels found in the same source, in the same *Grundschrift*, or in the same stratum are considered, and then—in the second, third, and fourth places—consideration is given to parallels which occur in approximately contemporary literature, in earlier literature, and in later literature. In this way, in a given case, one should hold in view not only related and contrasting parallel concepts but also their persistence within a particular genre, giving special attention to nuances in a concept, which may arise when it is related now with one, now with another genre. Methods used in the study of the history of ideas and of the history of tradition must be freely adapted and applied here so that the precise meaning of a concept within the text under consideration may be grasped as exactly as possible. To be sure, one must not become so absorbed in the historical investigation that one overlooks the meaning of the immediate context, which may be decisive.[52a] If parallels can be adduced from non-Israelite history, religion, or culture, one's results may have to be modified or may take on special significance—a fact which is also important for subject exegesis.

We come now to the question of the resources at our disposal. It scarcely needs to be emphasized explicitly that Bible dictionaries[53] and works on Old Testament theology[54] can be used with profit in concept exegesis. However, this is the appropriate place to recommend the *Theological Dictionary of the New Testament*,[55] which, at least for the central concepts, traces the prehistory of the New Testament in the Old Testament and for this reason is an indispensable resource for Old Testament exegesis as well. In independent scientific work the consultation of this should, once again, be postponed until one's own investigation has been completed. No one who works scientifically is spared the realization that our fathers saw just as much as and often more than we do. However, whoever becomes accustomed to depending on the work of others not only lays a poor foundation for the asking of new and original questions but also deprives himself of the methodological experience necessary for future work.

Once again the beginner finds his primary orientation in regard to the religious environment of the Old Testament in Noth, *The Old Testament World*.[56] The *Kulturgeschichte des Alten Orients: Mesopotamien, Hethiterreich, Syrien-Palästina, Urartu*, edited by H. Schmökel with the collaboration of H. Otten, V. Maag, and Th. Beran,[57] and the *World of the Old Testament* by C. H. Gordon[58] should also be mentioned here. Similar assistance is provided, from the special points of view indicated in their titles, by the works of W. F. Albright, *From the Stone Age to Christianity: Monotheism and the Historical Process*,[59] and *Archeology and the Religion of Israel*.[60] Whoever wishes to experience something of the understanding of life that was characteristic of the ancient oriental religions will take up first of all the fine book of H. and H. A. Frankfort, J. A. Wilson, and Thorkild Jacobsen, *The Intellectual Adventure of Ancient Man*,[61] in addition to which—partly for supplementation and partly for correction of what is said there about the Mesopotamian relationships—we may mention the essay, "Altmesopotamisches Lebensgefühl,"[62] by F. R. Kraus. As an introduction to Egyptian religion there may be named, in addition to H. A. Frankfort's *Ancient Egyptian Religion*[63] or J. Vandier's *La Religion Égyptienne*,[64] above all S. Morenz's *Ägyptische Religion;*[65] H. Kees's *Ägypten*[66] and H. Bonnet's *Reallexikon der ägyptischen Religionsgeschichte*[67] may be named as a good cultural history and a more detailed reference work, respectively. An introduction to Canaanite literature, religion, and culture, as these are revealed in the texts discovered at Ras Shamra (Ugarit), is given by J. Gray, *The Legacy of Canaan: The Ras Shamra Texts and Their Relevance to the Old Testament.*[68] Since the linguistic differences between Hebrew and Ugaritic are not such that they prohibit the discovery of parallel words and expressions, explicit reference may be made to the grammar, dictionary, and texts in a comprehensive *Ugaritic Manual* by C. H. Gordon.[69] Among the available translations of the Ugaritic texts are C. H. Gordon's *Ugaritic Literature: A Comprehensive Translation of the Poetic and Prose Texts,*[70] H. L. Ginsberg's *Ugaritic Myths, Epics, and Legends,*[71] G. R. Driver's *Canaanite Myths and Legends,*[72] O. Aistleitner's *Die mythologischen und kultischen Texte aus Ras Schamra,*[73] and A. Jirku's *Kanaanäische Mythen und Epen aus Ras Schamra-Ugarit.*[74] A comprehensive survey of the history, culture, and religion of the Hittites is provided by A. Goetze's *Kleinasien.*[75] The work of E. Dhorme and R. Dussaud, *Les religions de Babylonie et d'Assyrie; Les religions des Hittites et des Hourrites, des Phéniciens et des Syriens,*[76] deals with the religions of the Semitic peoples of both east and west, as well as with the religion of the Hittites; the volume *Religionsgeschichte des Alten Orients* in the *Handbuch der Orientalistik*[76a] has much the same scope.

For the Mesopotamian field B. Meissner's *Babylonien und Assyrien* (two volumes)[77] may still be used with profit. In this connection we may also mention the illustrated atlases, whose importance, as their titles indicate, is by no means limited to the study of the history of religions. The *Altorientalische Bilder zum Alten Testament* by H. Gressmann[78] and the *Ancient Near East in Pictures* by J. B. Pritchard[79] may be regarded as the standard works, and these have won attention far beyond the Old Testament field. In addition to M. A. Beek's excellent *Bildatlas der assyrisch-babylonischen Kultur*[80] we may mention the more specialized contributions of M. Riemschneider, H. Schmökel, W. Wolf, H. H. von der Osten, and A. Jirku, dealing with the Hittites, Ur, Asshur and Babylon, the world of the Egyptians, of the Persians, and of the Old Testament; these appear in the series, *Grosse Kulturen der Frühzeit*.[81] Note may be made here of two textbooks of the history of religion, both of which bear the title, *Christus und die Religionen der Erde;* one, in two volumes, is by Chantepie de la Saussaye (4th edition edited by A. Bertholet and E. Lehmann, 1925);[82] the other, in three volumes, is that edited by F. König.[83]

Finally, the exegete will examine the separate details and combinations of details again and again for the phenomena which are manifested in them, the basic structures of religious experience and behavior; for this purpose he will need to make use of *Religion in Essence and Manifestation,* by G. van der Leeuw[84] or of *Formenwelt des Religiösen* by K. Goldammer.[85] The phenomenological approach facilitates the comparison and understanding of phenomena which are apparently or actually quite different, since it involves sifting through the multiplicity of concrete details for the fundamental ways of behavior underlying them. Explicit warning must be given of the danger of being misled by structural similarities into overlooking radical differences which can arise between phenomena that at first run entirely parallel, since the whole range of ideas about the meaning of life may be divided by profound dissimilarities. The existence of this danger, which is recognized by all leading scholars in the field of religion, does not justify a final verdict about the method as such.[86] In my opinion, there can be no doubt that the phenomenological approach offers definite assistance in constructing a bridge from a text belonging to the distant past to the living questions it reflects. Since every understanding of alien thought processes rests, in the final analysis, on arguments based on anal-

ogy, the understanding of human utterances is facilitated
and methodologically ensured by an existential interpretation to the degree to which they appear alien in the first
place, owing to their concrete, historical embodiment of
ideas. In consequence of the common basic structure of
mankind, we can gain some understanding of the unusual
if we can compare it with our own modern ways of behavior
and our own interpretations of the universe; we are thus
compelled to go further and to ask whether and with what
right those past evidences of committed human existence,
which are dealt with in all religious documents, can put our
own conduct and our own understanding of ourselves and
of our world in question. Only at this point has the exegesis
reached its proper goal, since, as *biblical* exegesis, it is concerned to make us, today, aware of the claim which the past
evidence has upon us. In our procedure we shall in fact
separate existential interpretation from concept exegesis
proper and deal with it together with or following context
exegesis.

In context exegesis all previous exegetical steps make
their contribution, directly or indirectly. Textual criticism
has only established the text which must now be explained
in its internal nuances. Literary criticism has revealed its
stratification into different levels in the course of the preparatory structural analysis, together with the internal relationship of the separate "scenes" or parts of the narrative.
Form criticism has determined the genre, the distinctive
linguistic features, and the *Sitz im Leben*. Moreover, the
stylistic analysis has already given a preliminary but important indication of the author's purpose. The references to
persons, circumstances of time and place, and other details,
which were unintelligible at the start, were explained in subject exegesis. Concept exegesis has thrown light on the intellectual presuppositions that are taken for granted in the
text and thereby also "the background from which the ex-

pression under consideration has emerged."[87] In context exegesis all these preparatory steps need to be kept in mind; and now, in the continuing exposition, in which the text under consideration is, as it were, made to live again, they find their consummation. Only when the work of detailed analysis is followed by a genuinely vital synthesis can the work of exegesis be regarded as finished. Whether the exegete crowns his labors with an existential interpretation or with the establishment of the *skopos* or aim of a text will depend largely on the characteristics of the text under consideration. The interpreter must always be on guard against reading too much or too little into a text: on the one hand, he should take care not to impose a theological interpretation on a profane text, and on the other, he should not prematurely declare a religious text to be of no value. In this connection it must be pointed out that a text which in and of itself is profane has, as a result of having been imbedded in a larger narrative context or even by the mere fact of its reception into the canon of the Old Testament, received a theological significance which it is in every case essential to discover. And thus it appears that not only the investigation of the context, of the relationship of the subject matter of a text to the material which precedes and follows, but also its canonical position can provide an important contribution to the complete understanding of the text and its history.

VII. The Old Testament and Christian Theology

The Old Testament is primarily the Holy Scripture of the synagogue. Historical critical exegesis has, behind every secondary understanding of the text, sought to recover its original sense. On the threshold of systematic thought, exisential interpretation has discovered the self-understanding of the author—so far as such a thing admits of discovery—or of the community, in whose spiritual and intellectual life he has been nurtured. For the evaluation of the claim raised in the text, the way in which the exegete understands himself is in the last analysis decisive; that is, whether he thinks of himself as under God, the Lord of the future, which is not at his disposal, or as having the world at his own disposal. The biblical text will call him to the former self-understanding. As a Christian he will, to be sure, have to ask how the claim raised by the word of the Old Testament is related to the *one* Word of God witnessed to in the New Testament, that which was manifested in Jesus Christ. The Christian theologian, therefore, must view the witness of the Old Testament in the light of that of the New Testament, and the witness of the New Testament, in turn, in the light of the history of the Church and the ensuing formulation of creedal statements, which will assist him in finding the true center of Scripture. But since creeds and confessions themselves always need to have their scripturality tested anew by Scripture, it is clear that something more and something other is involved here than a formalistic examination, in which our Old Testament text functions, as it were, as the accused, upon which a verdict is to be pronounced on the basis of the New Testament and the creeds. On the basis of the New Testament and the creeds it will surely be possible to arrive at a practical critique of certain Old Testament notions in their original form.

One can only be warned against a premature understanding of the Old Testament in accordance with a traditional schema, perhaps that of the Old Testament as "law" and the New Testament as "gospel," or a formal one of the Old Testament as "promise" and the New Testament as "fulfillment." As a matter of principle one should venture to say No to the Old Testament only when the full meaning of Yes is understood. Whoever does not arrive at this understanding should call his own theology into question rather than the Old Testament, since the God of Jesus Christ was the God of Abraham, Isaac, and Jacob (Mark 12:26 f.) The unity of the people of God in time will make itself manifest, beyond the changes in ideas and institutions, in the *one* faith in God as the ground of the possibility and necessity of our being.

So much should be clear: Only a survey of the whole history of religious belief and only a survey of theology as a scholarly discipline, which here make their ultimate unity known, allow the word that has been brought to light by historical criticism to be transformed into the binding word that must be proclaimed today in the name of the Father and of the Son and of the Holy Ghost. Whether the Spirit actually stands behind the word for which this claim is made no method can ensure or by any means compel, since the Spirit "bloweth where it listeth" (John 3:8). Whoever knows that he is dependent on the testimony of the fathers of the faith so that he may bear witness rightly to the living God, knows, therefore, that the event which the word attests is not itself attainable; but also, at the same time, he knows that this knowledge does not release him from the task of interpreting, and thus actualizing, the testimony of the fathers. Or, to put it another way, whoever rejects the interpretation afforded by historical criticism denies the historicity of the revelation in Jesus Christ, whose God was the God of Abraham, Isaac, and Jacob.[88]

Werner Georg Kümmel

❖ ❖ ❖

NEW TESTAMENT EXEGESIS

The Point of View in Exegesis

Anyone who is interested in the exegesis of a New Testament text must be clear in his own mind about what it is that he wants to achieve. One can, in principle, approach the New Testament just as one can approach any other written tradition, from various perspectives: "an interpretation is . . . always oriented toward a specific way of asking questions, toward a specific point of view."[1] In the context of this introduction, it is true, we shall take for granted that a number of the possible ways of raising questions that are in themselves important are as a rule of no interest to the beginner or have significance only for specialists (e.g., the questions raised by specialists in grammar, historical linguistics, or the history of ideas). On the other hand, even a beginner who has no such specialized interests must keep clearly in mind which of two obvious ways of asking questions he will use in dealing with a particular exegetical problem, inasmuch as the following two ways of approaching a problem may be adopted as easily by the theological student as by the advanced exegete, especially in regard to the New Testament:

a) I intend, by scientific exegesis, to learn from the text what it says about the historical circumstances at the time of its composition, about its author and the readers for whom it was intended, about the intellectual milieu from which it originates, about the external or internal history of primitive Christianity, etc.

b) I intend, by scientific exegesis, to discover the objective meaning of the text, i.e., to learn from the text what it says about the subject matter discussed in it, and what this means for me personally.

These two approaches are equally legitimate, and the historical point of view is certainly not admissible only for historians and philologists. Work on the history of primitive Christianity, on the biography of Paul, on questions about the origin and interrelationship of the New Testament Scriptures, etc., is also indispensable for the theologian, for the understanding of primitive Christianity and the individual New Testament books. This point must be emphasized, however, because the recognition of the fundamental justification of *both* approaches must not be wrongly understood to imply that questions about the subject matter of a text can be answered *directly*. It is essential, rather, for all exegetical work on the New Testament, to understand that questions about the subject matter of a New Testament text can be answered only by way of a historical investigation of the text. Even if I do not mean to inquire explicitly about the grammar or about the historical or religious background of a passage under consideration, I cannot evade questions from these points of view if I wish to answer questions about the subject matter of the text reliably. The meaning of the subject matter of the text and, therefore, its meaning for me can open up for me only if I have understood what the text was intended to say, in accordance with the purpose of its author, to the readers he first had in view—in his and their language. Every kind of subject exegesis is an interpretation of the text itself, and not an arbitrary violation of the text, only if it attempts to bring the historical meaning of the text, in its historical context, to new life. For of itself the ancient text is mute, and only by scientific scholarly effort can it be made to speak again, at least in some measure.

1. Text of the New Testament— Textual Criticism

To facilitate the discussion of further methodological procedures, I shall assume from now on that the question the student means to put to the text is, generally speaking, that which is concerned with the meaning of the subject matter of the text. In view of the nature of the New Testament Scriptures, which we have briefly indicated above, this question can be answered only by moving step by step toward the recovery of the original meaning of a text. Presupposed for this gradual process of recovery of the meaning of a text is, of course, the knowledge of the text itself, in its original wording.

The fact that we have at our disposal, in E. Nestle's and K. Aland's edition of the Greek New Testament,[2] a reliable and widely recognized "average text" must not lead us to the mistaken idea that the Nestle text can be accepted as the original text without further ado. Rather, the student must be clear on two points: (a) The text of Nestle's edition is a mechanically produced average text based on the scholarly editions in use at the end of the nineteenth century. Even though this mechanically created text has recently been altered in a few places (e.g., in John 1:21) contrary to this principle, it does not by any means always reflect the critical opinions of its editors. The Nestle text is not *intended* to be correct in every place. (b) To make proper use of the Nestle text one must re-examine the critical apparatus again and again, and hence the beginner must, as soon as possible, with the help of the introduction to the Nestle edition, acquire a knowledge of the symbols and abbreviations employed in textual criticism. Indeed, the ability to read the apparatus is still not sufficient to enable one to judge the value of the attestation of a variant reading; for this, one must know something of the history of the text and some of the most important rules for deciding questions in textual criticism. Whoever is unable to become acquainted with the fundamentals of textual criticism from a lecture or lectures on the subject should, therefore, as soon as possible, work carefully through a short exposition of the subject.[3]

The knowledge of textual criticism gained in this way can, to be sure, be applied only in connection with exegesis itself, and it is quite inexpedient to try to establish a text from the point of view of textual criticism at the start, independently of exegesis, though this is exactly what beginners like to do. It is therefore recommended that one school one's judgment in the use of textual criticism, while engaged in exegesis, by thinking through each decision for or against variants offered in the apparatus even if they are not essential for understanding the text (no example of such variants can be considered in what follows).

II. Linguistic Resources

The second indispensable step in recovering the original meaning of a text is to strive for a *linguistic* understanding, i.e., for a correct translation of the text. A knowledge of the vocabulary is not enough to enable one to translate the text, though this is naturally presupposed. Whoever wishes to translate a New Testament text that is not at first completely intelligible (e.g., Mark 15:26) must be informed (*a*) about the various possible meanings of the ambiguous words and (*b*) about the various possible meanings of the grammatically ambiguous constructions involved. From this it is clear that for working out a correct translation both a dictionary and a grammar are indispensable. Since the Greek used by the authors of the New Testament is no longer the classical language but a variety of Hellenistic Greek, one must always take account of the possibility that a change may have taken place in the use of a word or of a grammatical construction. Further, if the student is to be aware of such changes and be informed about the range of possible meanings for a word, he must make an exhaustive survey of the occurrences of the word in its different meanings as well as of the various translations that have been proposed; for this reason he should avoid using school dictionaries, pocket dictionaries, "keys," and the like, all of which may be very useful in their proper place.

Concord

A comprehensive view of the whole of classical and Hellenistic Greek linguistic usage is furnished in the dictionary of Liddell and Scott, but such exhaustive information is normally unnecessary, and the dictionary which suffices for all ordinary purposes is that of W. Bauer (this the student should own, if possible).[4] The beginner should make it a rule to look up in Bauer's *Lexicon* all words whose meaning is not completely unambiguous and, circumstances permitting, should work through the other passages cited there and the bibliographical references as well, insofar as it seems useful to do so (looking up the references given by Bauer to parallels in the Apostolic Fathers or in late Jewish or secular literature can be very helpful in many cases). Similarly, grammatical questions which arise in translating, especially those dealing with syntax, cannot be answered fully with the help of an introductory grammar alone. The best resource here, which should be consulted rather than read, is the *Grammar of the Greek New Testament* by F. Blass and A. Debrunner, translated by R. Funk. A short

book by C. F. D. Moule is also very instructive, and may be
read with profit.[5] With these resources one can work out a
provisional translation, which must, of course, be confirmed
by the appropriate exegetical considerations. Indeed, modern scholarly translations (in commentaries or separately
published) may serve as controls for one's own translation,
but to use these before one has completed one's own exegesis is strongly to be discouraged, since otherwise it is easy
for one to neglect to make the sentence structure and the
different possibilities for translating the text really clear to
oneself, and far too easy for one to fail to see how uncertain
one or another proposed translation may be.

III. Questions of Introduction

If one wishes to understand a text in its original sense,
one must also be acquainted with the circumstances in
which the writing in which the text appears came into being. This information can be obtained only by investigating
the writing itself together with all other evidence about the
writing and its author. But, desirable as it may be for the
student to pursue such an investigation as an individual
project in the course of his study, perhaps in a seminar
report, it is impossible to carry out such an investigation by
oneself in every case; hence, in general, as a further preparatory step in interpreting a New Testament text, one
turns to the appropriate scholarly literature for information
on the so-called "questions of introduction" that concern
the writing under consideration.

Here there are three possibilities: (a) One may read
the introduction to a scientific commentary on the writing
concerned. It should be noted, however, that only the more
comprehensive introductions are adequate for this purpose (hence, perhaps, not those in *Das Neue Testament*

Deutsch), that not all commentaries have introductions which deal with these questions, and that the introductions in older commentaries can no longer serve this purpose, even if their exegesis still retains its value. (*b*) One may read the articles dealing with the writing in question in the major reference works (*RGG, LThK* [*IDB, HDB, EBi, HDCG, HDAC*, etc.; see p. 93 for key to abbreviations]), which are frequently very comprehensive and have good bibliographies; however, these articles do not in all cases undertake to survey the historical problems. (*c*) One may read the appropriate section in a standard "Introduction to the New Testament" textbook[6] and, if necessary, look up particular details in the specialized works mentioned in the bibliographies given there. Here it is important, not so much to be informed about all the problems presented by the New Testament book in question, as to be clear about the historical context and prehistory of the text to be interpreted. However, it is especially important to keep clearly in mind what can and what cannot be known with certainty, so that the exposition of the text is not based on mere suppositions as if they were assured results.

IV. The Task of Exegesis

After one has completed this preliminary general survey of the manuscript tradition, the problems of translation, and the historical uncertainties surrounding a text, one can proceed with the exegesis proper. This is the point at which a clear and careful answer must be given to the question mentioned at the outset: What do I want to achieve by my exegesis? For it is the aim which I have in view that will determine whether I concentrate my interest primarily on questions about the origin and historical context of a writing, on questions about its wider religious context and background, or on theological questions proper. For considerations of space, we shall confine ourselves to the single aim of searching out and interpreting the objective meaning of the text, and thereby also of gaining insight into the theological problems touched on in the text. Similar methodological considerations apply when the exegesis has other ends in view.

When we undertake to discover the objective meaning of a New Testament passage it is methodologically essential to differentiate between the Synoptic Gospels, on the one hand, and the remaining New Testament books, on the other.

a) For the majority of the New Testament books the essential task consists in investigating the meaning of the statements of the author of the writing in question and in setting the statements of individual passages in their context in the writing or corpus of writings concerned. Where we know that a literary relationship exists between texts we are studying (e.g., between Colossians and Ephesians, or Jude and 2 Peter), the consideration of this relationship can help us in our interpretation of the dependent writing only in that it enables us better to understand the special characteristics of a passage as it deviates from the original.

b) It is otherwise with the Synoptics. Here three or four steps are methodologically necessary if we wish to grasp the meaning of a text completely, particularly where Jesus' words, or stories about Jesus, are present (not, perhaps, for passages peculiar to the different evangelists, e.g., Luke 1:1-4 or Matthew 28:16-20).

1) First, we are confronted by the text in context as formulated by the evangelist, and we have to ask what the evangelist means to say in a particular passage in the context of his Gospel. That is, questions about the wording, the correct translation, etc., naturally arise first vis-à-vis the

Gospel as it lies before us, or as it can be established by textual criticism.

2) Even when the explanation of a Synoptic passage in the context of the Gospel concerned does not lead to questions incapable of being answered on the basis of *this* context, we cannot, when dealing with Matthew and Luke, leave out of account the fact that they have a large part of their subject matter in common with Mark and a further part in common with each other. To be sure, the solution of the Synoptic Problem is still not entirely settled, but it is just here that one must be quite clear—at least in theory and in general—about questions of introduction which are relevant for the passage being interpreted, if one wishes to give an adequate interpretation for a Synoptic text. Even if one does not accept the two-source theory,[7] which is presupposed in the following discussion, one must try to explain the literary relationship between the Synoptics somehow, and take account of this explanation in one's exegesis. The second step of the exegetical task here, therefore, is to inquire further about the sources which are extant or which may be conjectured to underlie two Gospels, and which make the form of the text as we have it more or less easy to understand.

3) Behind the literary sources that are extant or that may be inferred, however, lies the *oral tradition,* which took shape in the believing community. This insight of the form-critical school[8] is generally accepted today, even if widely varying inferences are drawn from it. Exegesis should, however, by no means seek to discover only the theological significance of a tradition in the context of a Gospel, but to press forward to the form of the tradition as the evangelist himself received it. Further, this form lies either directly behind the text as we received it (as in Mark or in the special sources of Matthew or Luke) or behind the sayings-source

(commonly referred to as Q), which may be inferred to underlie parts of Matthew and Luke.

4) Whether it is the task of the exegete to take still another step further back and to ask about the form of the saying on the lips of Jesus or of the account which goes back to the life of Jesus, or to decide *whether* the saying or account does in fact go back to the historical Jesus, is disputed. Whoever (like the author of this essay[9]) gives an affirmative answer here will regard it as the last part of the task of interpreting a Synoptic text to ask also about the meaning and form of a saying or account in its oldest attainable form, and about its relationship to the proclamation of the Gospel and to the work of Jesus.

V.   Resources for Exegesis

Apart from the somewhat different approach required in the study of Synoptic texts, which we have discussed above, exegetical procedure is the same for all texts. The methodological ideal in interpreting a text is to interpret it as a component part of a larger whole; hence, in a measure, interpreting a text involves the interpretation of the whole writing. Although it is very desirable for every student to work through a whole New Testament book exegetically— or, indeed, through more than one—this ideal cannot always be realized in practice. Hence the two following presuppositions must be strictly observed, even if one intends to work through only a small portion of a book:

a) The beginning and end of a section must be carefully defined (the demarcation of the traditional ecclesiastical "pericopes" is often very questionable!), because an individual sentence or idea can be made intelligible only in relation to its own narrow context.

b) Therefore the *wider* context of a section to be interpreted must be kept in view, so that one can recognize the
sense of an individual idea within this context and from this
can correctly perceive the boundaries of the section in which
it occurs. To be sure, one cannot take it for granted that a
sentence which has come down to us in a particular context
can be recognized as having belonged to that context originally. Even if this is assumed as a working hypothesis, it
does not always prove to be true, and where no train of
thought or logically intelligible relationship can be seen, the
connection should not be forced (cf., e.g., the series of sayings in Mark 9:48-50 or a paraenetic text like Romans
12:9-21).

The student cannot undertake the demarcation of a
section of the text and the examination of its wider context,
however, without referring to commentaries or specialized
works. Hence an important prerequisite for beginning the
work of exegesis is the selection of suitable exegetical aids.
Here the student must be warned against a double error. On
the one hand, many beginners are inclined to consult as
many commentaries as possible, especially if they are read-
ily accessible in a seminary library, in a seminar room, etc.,
and they will then easily be confused or altogether repelled
by the fullness of contradictory opinions. Some beginners,
on the other hand, content themselves with a single commentary known or recommended to them, and thus they
gain no adequate insight into the many-sidedness of the
problems that can arise. Although for really scientific work
one should make as comprehensive use of the literature as
possible, those who are just beginning study of this kind
will be well advised to limit themselves to two or three commentaries of different types.

No hard and fast rule can be given for selecting these

commentaries. The student should acquaint himself with the important series of commentaries and be aware of their characteristic peculiarities so that he will know where he can expect to find particular kinds of information; however, all of the important commentaries do not belong to any one series, and one must keep oneself informed as to what commentaries are available by referring to the most recent of them and to the newest textbooks on New Testament introduction. The selection one makes for oneself, then, will have to be guided by the professor's recommendations or by the experience of one's fellow students, or even by one's own tentative browsing. To be sure, one must not think that assistance in exegesis is to be found only in the commentaries on the New Testament book being studied; specialized works or essays frequently contain at least as extensive and helpful exegetical explanations, and one should allow oneself to be led to these special works by the references in recent commentaries, in Bauer's *Lexicon,* in the *Theological Dictionary of the New Testament,* or in articles in other works of reference.

Whenever the subject matter demands it, one can and must refer to specialized works on exegesis in addition to commentaries. Generally speaking, the commentaries are adequate to enable one to determine the boundaries of a section of the text and to discover its subdivisions, if any, and also to solve many isolated exegetical problems; however, for a deeper understanding of the more important concepts and their intellectual context one requires information about the history of ideas and about the more general interrelations of religious and theological thought. For dealing with such questions the most important and indispensable resource is a *concordance.* While for some kinds of work complete concordances are necessary,[10] for most purposes the abridged concordance of O. Schmoller[11] is sufficient;

this book should be in the hands of every theological student. With the help of a concordance one can make a preliminary survey of the use of a word or word-group within a writing, in a group of writings, in the writings of a single author, or in the whole New Testament, and from this one can at once gain important insights. However, if one wishes to put these insights in their historical context, one must make use of other special works, in particular the *Theological Dictionary of the New Testament.*[12] It must be admitted that the articles of this dictionary vary considerably in comprehensiveness and quality, and one cannot always be sure of finding needed information in it; however, as a rule, the bibliographies subjoined to the individual articles supply further assistance. The student will be well advised not to consult an article of the *TDNT* only where it touches on a text in which he is interested at the time, but whenever possible to read the whole article, since without information about the historical, religious, and conceptual background of a word or an idea, explanations about a single passage cannot be fully understood. The *TDNT* gives no information about names and concepts which do not belong to theology or to the history of ideas, so that for information about these one must consult the appropriate technical dictionaries as well as larger general works of reference.[13]

After assembling the necessary information with the help of the resources mentioned above and after surveying the various problems and the possibilities for their solution, the student can now himself approach a text and try his hand at an interpretation. Of course it is not necessary to follow the sequence of questions as they are given in this methodological sketch; how one approaches a text depends on the nature of the text itself. The main thing is for all of the questions to be taken into account. Further, at every point where it does not seem possible to reach a more or less certain conclusion, it is important not to conceal this fact from oneself; a not inconsiderable number of New Testament texts provide no really firm basis for the proclamation of the gospel, much less for the definition of doctrine. The assumption that every text *has* to be preached from is false for two reasons:

a) There are numerous "profane" texts in the New Testament, which contain no "kerygma" of any kind, and which can be made the basis of an existential address only by artificially allegorizing them or by treating them as mere "springboards" from which one sets out but to which one never returns (e.g., Mark 6:19-28; Acts 19:23-40).

b) There are theologically significant texts that resist all exegetical efforts to interpret them with certainty, and the exegete as well as the preacher should guard against pretending—for himself and for others—to a certainty which cannot be attained (e.g., Romans 11:25 f., 32; John 2:1-11). This warning is not intended to encourage the beginner to break off his exegetical work too soon; however, no one can make proper use of the methodological tool kit of pure exegesis unless he understands its limitations and learns to reserve judgment where no certain conclusions may be drawn.

In the following two sections of this chapter, the method of exegesis will be illustrated in the treatment of two passages; for neither of these is a complete commentary offered, and the exegetical viewpoint presented is not peculiarly my own, but one that is intentionally designed to serve as a methodological model. It should be taken for granted that the texts discussed here involve still other questions and that there are still other solutions besides the ones mentioned here.

VI. Interpretation of Romans 5:1-11

For the interpretation of Romans 5:1-11, I have chosen the commentaries of H. Lietzmann, O. Michel, and O. Kuss because they place three differing points of view at our disposal: Lietzmann's approach is that of philology and the history of religions, Michel's is more definitely theological, and Kuss's work is representative of modern Roman Catholic biblical scholarship.[14] As far as this text is concerned, questions of introduction may be taken as settled: the Epistle to the Romans is at all events the latest of the major letters of Paul and was written at the end of his so-called third missionary journey. The original unity of Romans, chapters 1-15, is also not in dispute. We can, therefore, proceed on the assumption that Romans 5:1-11 is to be understood as a component part of the train of thought developed in Romans, chapters 1-15.[15] Most commentators agree that the exposition of the theme of Romans 1:16 ff. (the righteousness of God is revealed for those who believe in the gospel) is concluded with 4:25; some scholars, it is true, understand 5:1-11 as continuing the preceding train of thought, and others feel that no new thought is introduced until 6:1.[16] However, Michel shows convincingly that after the creedlike conclusion in 4:23-25 the train of thought takes a new turn in 5:1; chapters 5-8 deal with the new life from God on the *basis* of the revelation of righteousness in the gospel. Thus the section 5:1-11 presupposes the exposition in 1:16-4:25, but it also introduces a new development in the thought. The end of the section is also clearly marked: still another thought is introduced in 5:12 (the certainty of the eschatological gift of life and righteousness is surer than the sure expectation of death). Romans 5:1-11 can therefore be considered by itself as a clearly defined section.

A preliminary survey of the section shows that three thoughts follow one another: verses 1-5 speak of peace with God, of the hope of glory, and of the situation of the Christian which is characterized by these; verses 6-8 point to the death of Jesus as the reason for this situation; verses 9-11 connect both of these ideas: through the death of Jesus our eschatological hope of salvation has become a certain hope (cf. Michel, especially). It is important to establish the sequence of the individual ideas and, hence, of the subdivisions of the section to be interpreted, because only in this way can the internal relationships of the interconnected single thoughts be understood and be put to service in exegesis.

The first subsection, verses 1-5, brings together three statements: (*a*) having been justified, we have peace with God and access to grace; (*b*) hence, we exult in our sufferings on the basis of our hope; (*c*) this hope receives its power from the Spirit, which has been given to us. The first statement must be based on what precedes, since it is connected with the preceding material by *oun:* the justification described in 3:21-4:25, which has been given to believers, is the basis for maintaining that *eirēnē echomen*. This reading of the present Nestle text was, as the symbol ⦿ in the apparatus indicates, accepted into the text only since the seventeenth edition, contrary to the mechanical principles on which it is based, because the majority of commentators regard this reading as original. Kuss, however, with others, still defends the reading *echōmen*, which stood in earlier editions of Nestle.

A decision for one reading rather than the other will obviously affect the sense of the passage quite materially, so that the first business of the interpreter here is to make this textual decision. Reference to the apparatus and to Lietzmann's commentary reveals that the subjunctive is substantially better attested; except for later corrections of Codex

Vaticanus and Codex Sinaiticus, the indicative is probably to be found only in a fragment of the fourth century (0220) and in manuscript G (Codex Boernerianus), which belongs to the so-called "Western" text, and in addition in a few Latin witnesses: hence, in sum, only in some Western witnesses since the fourth century (the commentary of Ambrosiaster belongs to this period; this should be looked up in a lexicon!). On the other hand, this reading is not found in any of the "Egyptian" witnesses. Therefore, according to the rules of textual criticism, the subjunctive would have to be regarded as original (it is better attested, since it is found in the generally preferable "Egyptian" text and also in some manuscripts of the "Western" text). However, if one tries to interpret this reading, it must be understood as an exhortation to maintain (or to establish?) peace with God through the mediation of Jesus Christ. Thus it is already unclear what *echōmen* really means in this instance, and this exhortation does not fit at all well with the continuation in verse 2, which describes the access to God's grace as a gift that has been received. An examination of the immediate context takes us no further. However, the weakly attested variant *echomen* is still an ancient one (even Codex G reflects an older text), so that the possibility of its correctness should be tested by an investigation of Paul's use of *eirēnē*.

Since the three commentaries we are using do not help us here,[17] we turn to Schmoller's concordance.[18] Here we find that Paul can indeed use *eirēnē* of the relation of human beings to one another, but that in general, where *eirēnē* describes the relation of mankind to God, *God* appears as the originator of *eirēnē*. For confirmation of this survey of Pauline linguistic usage, we refer to the article on *eirēnē* in *TDNT* (II, 415; W. Foerster), where it is pointed out that a few verses further on, in Romans 5:10, it is said that men were enemies of God and that God reconciled them to him-

self through the death of His Son. Thus, it should be clear that the weakly attested reading *echomen,* in spite of its weak attestation, must be correct (and we can learn from Lietzmann and Foerster how the early origin of the incorrect reading can perhaps be explained). Still another textual decision must be made before we can translate verses 1-2 with assurance: do the words *tēi pistei,* which are bracketed in Nestle's text, belong in the text or not? Here again, the commentaries disagree; Lietzmann gives good grounds for regarding the words as original, and they are also very well attested, but it is difficult to decide the question with certainty. However, it is not of great importance for the exegesis, because the role of faith in man's reception of righteousness has already been emphasized in verse 1. In any event, these two textual problems which we have briefly considered here will help to make clear to the beginner that, in spite of all the progress which has been made in textual criticism, there are still many variants which are fundamental for a clear understanding of individual texts, and yet which cannot be either accepted or rejected with complete certainty.

After these preliminary textual questions have been settled, the translation of verses 1-2 offers no special difficulty. Nevertheless, Lietzmann warns at verse 2, "One must beware of pressing the *kai* before *tēn prosagōgēn,*" and thus makes us aware of a logical difficulty presented by the usual translation, "by whom also we have access" ([AV; RSV has "through whom also . . ."] Kuss, Michel: "durch den wir auch den Zugang haben"): the grace in which we stand has not been made accessible to us by Christ *among others.* If we turn to Bauer's *Lexicon* for light on this difficulty, we find, under *kai,* II, 6, the information that *kai,* in combination with the relative pronoun, lends greater independence to the relative clause (Romans 9:24 is adduced, correctly, to substantiate this point). We should, therefore, probably not translate the *kai* in Romans 5:2 at all, or, possibly, render it by "indeed."[19] Paul thus infers from the gift of righteousness which is experienced in faith that, through Christ, peace with God is established for Christians and access to this grace is created as a reality of the existence of those who believe.[20]

This statement is now qualified by verses 2b-5. With a simple *kai,* which conceals for the moment the logic of his thought, Paul adds: *kauchōmetha ep'elpidi tēs doxēs tou theou,* and follows this with another *kauchōmetha,* introduced by one of his favorite phrases, *ou monon de.* A glance at the concordance shows at once that Paul frequently (as in verse 3) attaches the object or cause of boasting to *kauchasthai* with *en.* The combination of *kauchasthai* with *epi* (as in verse 2b), on the other hand, is not found elsewhere in Paul (nor, for that matter, in the whole New Testament). Bauer's *Lexicon* tells us, however, that this combination does occur in profane Greek as well as in the Greek Old Testament,[21] so that the change of prepositions in verses 2b-3 seems to be merely stylistic. Thus Paul limits the "possession" of Christ's gift of grace first by referring to the eschatological glory of God which is still to be revealed in its fullness; the Christian's hope of receiving this glory is perfectly certain, and therefore he can boast in hope.[22] To this future glory Paul contrasts the present reality of Christian existence, which consists in *thlipsis.* Another glance at the concordance shows that Paul uses this word to mean "affliction" in a very broad sense, personal and universally human as well as specifically Christian affliction (cf. Kuss). But this affliction which every Christian suffers is for Paul not a cause for complaining, but for boasting, because *thlipsis* gives rise to endurance, to character, and to hope which does not disappoint. The commentaries point out that Paul is here using the rhetorical form of the sorites (or "chain-syllogism") to express the paradox that it is *thlipsis* which strengthens the Christian's hope for the coming glory. To understand this thought objectively one will first investigate the Pauline sense of *kauchasthai,* making use of the information in *TDNT* (III, 648 ff.; R. Bultmann; cf., however, also the excursus by Kuss, 219 ff.), and, second, one will bear in mind the fundamental proposition of verse 5*b*. For this to be understood the meaning of the genitive in the construction *hē agapē tou theou* must be clear as well as the meaning of the "outpouring of the love of God into our hearts through the Holy Spirit."

The concordance shows that Paul uses the phrase *hē agapē tou theou* very infrequently (Romans 8:39, 2 Corinthians 13:13), but refernce to Romans 5:8 and to the commentaries shows that in verse 5 Paul can only mean God's love toward us (and in the other two passages it is the same). The commentaries also indicate that the figure of the outpouring of the Holy Spirit is from the Old Testament, but that Paul varies it here so that the love of God is poured out, through the Spirit, into our hearts, by which he can only mean the certainty of God's love, which the Christian has received with the gift of the Spirit (cf. Michel). What Paul means by the "giving of the Holy Spirit" cannot, in fact, be learned from our passage, and it is plain that the expression can be made intelligible only if other Pauline expressions about the gift of the Spirit to Christians are compared with it. Here again a glance at the concordance is instructive (pointing, perhaps, to the parallels in 2 Corinthians 1:22; 5:5; 1 Thessalonians 4:8; Romans 8:11, 23; 1 Corinthians 3:16; 6:11), but in view of the fact that a definite doctrine of the Spirit permeates the whole Pauline theology, it is advisable to refer at this point to a comprehensive discussion of Paul's views on the subject.[23] Then the connection of the gift of the Spirit with faith, baptism, and the actions of Christians will be clear.

Paul's interest in Romans 5:5, to be sure, is not in the gift of the Spirit but in the love of God, for in elucidating this concept he adds verses 6-8. Here again the first question to be thrashed out is the textual one, viz., whether *ei ge* at the beginning of verse 6 is to be regarded as the correct reading (so Nestle), since the majority of the "Egyptian" witnesses and good "Western" witnesses read *eti gar*. The apparatus shows that the manuscript tradition on this point is very complex, so the beginner must turn to the commentaries, almost all of which accept *eti gar* as the original reading. However, if one does accept this opinion it remains uncertain how one should translate (cf. Kuss), and the only thing that is really clear is that Paul proves God's love for us with the statement that Christ died for the ungodly. And this meaning is confirmed by verse 8. In between, however, stands verse 7, the real *crux interpretum:* the first half of the sentence says that death on behalf of a righteous person hardly ever occurs (and, hence, it is implied that death on behalf of an unrighteous person *never* occurs, but the second half of the sentence states that death on behalf of a good person is entirely thinkable. Michel simply ignores this difficulty, and Lietzmann and Kuss, in different ways, accept the second clause as a Pauline self-correction of the first. This verse cannot really be explained with any certainty, and we can only infer from it that Paul intends, in verse 8, to describe the divine love as something scarcely conceivable among human beings.

With verse 9 Paul brings together the main ideas of the two preceding sections: "We are justified by the death of Jesus," and once again he derives the hope for final salvation from the reality of this divine act. The expression *dikaiōthentes en tōi haimati autou* is not intelligible without further ado. With the help of the concordance one will, therefore, examine Paul's use of prepositions with *dikaiō-thēnai* as well as his use of *haima,* and determine that Paul also connects *en* with *dikaioun* (Romans 3:4, 1 Corinthians 4:4, Galatians 3:11; 5:4), and by means of it indicates the facts which form the basis of justification. Further, the parallel use of *haima* in Romans 3:25, Colossians 1:20 shows that Paul uses *haima* as a sort of shorthand for "the death of Christ for our sins" (1 Corinthians 15:3).[24] For understanding verse 9 it is also important to be aware of Paul's frequent use of the argument *a minori ad maius* (Kuss and Michel may be consulted on this, and Michel's reference to Strack-Billerbeck should be looked up[25]). A comparison of Paul's argumentation with the rabbinic prototype will show that in Paul there is no exegetical drawing out of conclusions but, rather, an argument arising out of the certainty of faith, which draws its consequences from the justification that is known in experience.

This experience of justification Paul now reinterprets in verses 10 f. by means of the concept of atonement. To understand the meaning of this idea we first compare (using the concordance) the linguistic usage of *katallassō* and *katallagē,* and thus we find that only 2 Corinthians 5:18 f. offers a true parallel; after this we examine the context of Romans 5:9-11. As a result of these inquiries we see that for Paul the agent of atonement or reconciliation is God, just as He is also the agent of justification—which is, therefore, obviously the same thing. God effects the reconciliation of sinful, hostile mankind to himself and reconciles himself to them through the death of Christ; the fact of reconciliation must be preached and accepted, and when accepted it imparts a real participation in the life of the risen Christ. If we wish to have a more precise understanding of these ideas we will first investigate the origin of the concept of atonement. The commentaries do not help us here, but the *TDNT* (I, 254, F. Büchsel) and Strack-Billerbeck (III, 519) show that the idea is met in late Judaism, but only in relation to atoning actions or prayers directed by men *toward* God. Moreover, the reference books and works on Pauline theology[26] tell us that Paul radically altered this idea, and that for Paul God himself effects atonement and makes it available, and that He does this, paradoxically, through the devotion of His Son in death (Romans 8:32). It is important that one should be clear that Paul, in this presentation, *proclaims* the atoning work of God, but he attempts no explanation of it.

Paul completes his train of thought in verse 11 by describing this reality which has been received in faith, this God-given atonement, as the foundation for the Christians' boasting that was referred to in verse 3 (Michel correctly calls attention to the repeated *nun* in verses 9 and 11): to boast of affliction and to boast of reconciliation by God are, therefore, obviously identical. A final exegetical problem is offered by the formula "[we boast] through our Lord Jesus Christ." Since the concluding relative clause of verse 11 (*di'hou*, etc.) describes Christ unequivocally as the agent and cause of God's reconciling act, it seems hard to refer the immediately preceding formula ("through our Lord Jesus Christ") to Christ as the mediator of Christian boasting. Here further light is cast by Kuss's excursus, in which it is shown that Paul can use this formula in much the same way for the past as well as for the present saving act of God; it is therefore clear that we can boast by the help of the heavenly Lord God, because the Lord who died on the cross and rose again to heavenly life gives us the possibility of boasting, through His Spirit (5:5!).

When we have tried to solve the exegetical problems of

Romans 5:1-11 in the manner sketched here, the text should
be accessible to us so that we can now not only translate it
and understand the various concepts involved in it, but can
also consider it seriously, as addressed to us.

VII.   Exegesis of Matthew 12:22-37

As a second example, the exegesis of Matthew 12:22-
37 will illustrate the procedure to be followed with a Synoptic text. For commentaries on this text I choose Klostermann, Schniewind, and J. Schmid; and, in addition, the
commentaries on Mark by Lohmeyer, Taylor, and Grundmann; and those on Luke by Klostermann and Rengstorf.[27]
The commentaries on Mark and Luke must be consulted,
for whenever a Synoptic text has parallels in one or both of
the other Synoptics it is necessary to consider these parallels
also. In the exegesis of a Synoptic text it is therefore essential to take a Synopsis[28] as a point of departure and, in
every case, to determine whether Synoptic parallels are
present and whether they can contribute to the understanding of the text being interpreted.

There is no difficulty in determining the boundaries of
the Matthean section. The preceding summary statement
ends with 12:21, and the healing of the demoniac mentioned in 12:22 introduces the controversy about the power
behind Jesus' works. It is also clear that a new section
begins in 12:38, since the entrance of new parties to the
discussion is indicated. The analysis of the section also confirms at least the first of these boundaries (one should not
allow oneself to be misled by Huck's superscription before
12:25!). First, after the amazement of the crowd at Jesus'
healing the deaf and dumb man in verses 22-24, the Pharisees bring up the accusation that Jesus is in league with
demons; Jesus replies to this, making use of analogies

(verses 25 ff.) to show the absurdity of this charge, pointing out the proper relationship of opponents to each other (verse 27) and explaining the true meaning of his power over demons (verse 28). Here the introduction of evidence seems to be over, but in spite of this a further analogy is introduced in verse 29 as another argument showing the absurdity of the charge that Jesus is in league with demons; verse 30 is probably intended to show the application of this. With this, however, the refutation of the accusation is finally finished; the saying about blasphemy against the Son of man and the Holy Spirit in verse 31 is, indeed, introduced with *dia touto,* but it is far from clear what this is supposed to refer back to. The sayings about the tree and the fruit (verses 33-35) and about the necessity for giving an account for idle words (verses 36 f.) are even less obviously related to the foregoing discussion about being in league with demons, and no new beginning would be recognizable before verse 38, apart from the change in parties to the conversation. Thus the analysis shows that the section is obviously put together out of several independent component parts, and that therefore it should not be taken for granted that the author of Matthew's Gospel expected the reader to understand it as a coherent unity. An exegesis that is meant to interpret the text in the evangelist's sense will, therefore, on the basis of the analysis of the text itself, be limited to making each separate component part of the text intelligible by itself.

If the text to be interpreted does not belong to Matthew's special source, it is part of the exegetical task to take account of the parallels and to ask whether they can contribute anything to understanding the text; this is particularly true where Mark is to be supposed as a source for Matthew and Luke. Mark 3:22-30, which is parallel to Matthew 12:22-37, contains no account of a healing, but does begin with the charge about being in league with demons; Jesus shows the absurdity of this with the same analogies as in Matthew; however, the analogy of the Strong Man, which comes as a sort of afterthought or post-script in Matthew (12:29), follows without a break in Mark 3:27. Then follows in Mark 3:28 f. the statement that blasphemy against the Holy Spirit will not be forgiven, and here the addition of the saying is easily intelligible, since in verse 30 the blasphemy against the Holy Spirit is related to the charge of being in league with demons. With this the Marcan pericope ends; the sayings found in Matthew 12:23-37, whose connection with the charge of being in league with demons seemed so obscure, are, therefore, lacking in Mark. It goes without saying that if the Marcan text itself were being exegeted, one would have to ask whether it is not itself a composite section. In fact, this is quite probably true,[29] but this insight contributes nothing essential for understanding the Matthean text, since Matthew has obviously used this Marcan text which, by itself, forms an intelligible coherent unity.

However, in the present case the Lucan parallels must also be brought in, because a comparison of the wording shows that Luke is not dependent on Mark here, but has contacts with Matthew in those places where Matthew goes beyond Mark.[30] In Luke 11:14-23, the section dealing with the charge about being in league with demons appears not as a parallel to Mark 3:22 ff. (Luke leaves this pericope out), but in his "travel narrative," in connection with a series of controversies with the Pharisees (cf. Rengstorf); this already suggests that Luke is following another tradition here. Luke 11:14 f. begins the pericope, as does Matthew, with a demon exorcism and the crowd's amazed (or abusive) reaction to it. The refutation of the charge and the correct interpretation of the healing of demoniacs follow in verses 17-20, but the wording of these verses corresponds not to Mark, but to Matthew; Luke puts the saying about the Strong Man (Matthew 12:29), which in Matthew has the effect of a sort of afterthought, into the same context as it has in Matthew, but with different wording (verses 21 f.), and, like Matthew, adds the not entirely appropriate application of verse 23. With this the Lucan pericope ends. To be sure, Luke also has (in 12:10) a partial parallel to the Matthean (not the Marcan) form of the saying about blasphemy against the Son of man or against the Holy Spirit, and the sayings about the tree and the fruit occur in 6:43-45; however, both of these passages have quite different contexts.

The comparison of Matthew with Luke enables us to assert with confidence that Matthew 12:33-35 has in fact been taken over from another tradition and, even more confidently, to draw this conclusion about verses 36 f., which are found only in Matthew. For Matthew 12:22-32, however, the comparison with Mark *and* Luke shows that Matthew has contacts alternately with Mark and Luke and, therefore, it is in the highest degree probable that the author of Matthew has combined the parallel versions, found in Mark and Q, of the pericope about the accusation of being in league with demons with the sayings there appended to it, and has added to this combination a further group of sayings from Q and one saying from his own special source. (The student should check this hypothesis, advanced on the basis of his own observations in the Synopsis, by reading the relevant portions of the commentaries of Klostermann, Schmid, and Grundmann.)

From all of this a twofold conclusion follows for the exegesis of Matthew 12:22-37:

a) Whenever one cannot without difficulty recognize a chain of thought linking together the different component parts of a text, one must not assume that a connection exists; in such cases the primary purpose of the exegesis of a Synoptic Gospel, viz., the determination of the meaning which the evangelist has given to a text taken over by him, cannot be accomplished with complete certainty.

b) The individual component parts of the section must, of course, first be interpreted as they stand in Matthew's version, but we must always bear in mind that a comparison with Mark and Luke may enable us to recognize a more original version of the tradition, and this will occasionally take us nearer to the meaning of the saying on the lips of Jesus.

It is in the light of these considerations that we may now attempt to arrive at an understanding of the Matthean text. The introductory scene (verses 22-24) offers no exegetical difficulties. The healing of the demoniac is interpreted by the crowd as a possible indication of Jesus' messiahship, but by the Pharisees it is ascribed to the assistance of Beelzebul, the prince of demons. Since Luke 11:14 f. contains essentially the same material, this form of the introduction to the controversy probably comes from the sayings-source Q, so that nothing of Matthew's editorial purpose can be learned from it.[31] Jesus' answer begins in verses 25 f. with the two analogies of the kingdom and of the city or house, which cannot stand if they are divided internally; from these it is deduced that a division in Satan's kingdom would have a similar result. Comparison with Mark and Luke shows that Matthew is here following Q, in general, but that he has added the example of the house from Mark, without thereby introducing any material change. In order to understand the sense of this argument against the possibility of Satan's kingdom being divided, one must know what ideas about demons and Satan were current in the New Testament period. This information can best be obtained by reading the articles *daimōn* and *satanas* in *TDNT*,[32] where it is shown that Jesus, in contrast to Jewish tradition, sees the demon world as completely subject to Satan; thus he, in contrast to his opponents, regards an internecine struggle within Satan's kingdom as unthinkable. Jesus knows only the *one* question, namely, whether God *or* Satan is at work in an event, and we must be aware of this rigidly monistic view of the Satanic realm in order to understand the connection with the following verses in Matthew.

Two sayings follow, in Matthew 12:27 f., which Matthew has in common only with Luke, but the connection with what precedes is immediately obvious only for verse 27. The point of verse 27 is clear when one learns (e.g., from Klostermann) that Jesus takes for granted the existence of Jewish exorcists and that "your sons" means, in fact, "your people." Thus Jesus is arguing that the Pharisees' accusation is disproved because they raise it only against him and not also against the exorcists in their own numbers. Beside this, however, in verse 28, Matthew places a saying whose meaning raises difficulties. A glance at the concordance shows that the verb *phthanein* occurs in the Synoptics only in this saying, and, hence, also never occurs elsewhere in connection with *basileia tou theou*. Its meaning can therefore be learned only from its use elsewhere in the New Testament or in profane writers, and in all other New Testament passages (with the exception of 1 Thessalonians 4:15, where it means "anticipate, come ahead of time") the meaning is clearly "arrive" (Bauer's *Lexicon* and the commentaries confirm this).[33] The student will therefore have to find out whether this saying can mean that the exorcisms which Jesus performs by the power of God's Spirit are to be taken as an actualization of God's kingdom among his hearers. A glance at the otherwise verbally similar parallel in Luke 11:20 will show him that Luke has "by the finger of

God" instead of "in the Spirit of God," but this is hardly a
material difference (cf. Schniewind). Matthew therefore intends to say, whether he has the original version here or
not,[34] that Jesus is acting in the power of the Spirit of God
when he casts out demons (and the concordance shows that
Matthew has prepared for this understanding of Jesus' activity in 3:16; 4:1; and 12:18). But if Jesus is maintaining, in
verse 28, that his casting out demons through the working
of the Holy Spirit proves that the kingdom of God has come,
the connection of 12:28 to 12:27 can hardly be original,
since the juxtaposition of these two verses implies the doubt-
less unintentional result that the Pharisaic demon exorcisms
also prove the presence of God's kingdom.[35]

Evidently, then, two sayings, which do not belong together, were already combined in Q, and on this account
one will not be able to understand the Matthean text fully
without investigating the origin and original meaning of the
individual sayings. This further form-critical inquiry, however, leads one to ask whether the sayings belong to the
oldest traditions about Jesus and what meaning they had on
Jesus' lips (in the event that they do indeed come from
him). The exegete of such a Synoptic text must therefore
take these form-critical and historical questions into consideration if he wants to understand the text in the process of
its development and in the sense finally given to it by the
evangelist. If the commentaries give no bibliographical references to assist in following up such further questions, the
beginner will have to look up the references given in lexicons and dictionaries in the articles about Jesus, and he will
find, in the particular case we are dealing with, that the
meaning of Matthew 12:28, as arrived at on the basis of
New Testament linguistic usage, is regarded as doubtful by
many scholars, because it does not square well with other
sayings of Jesus about the *nearness* of God's kingdom, and

that for this reason one should understand *ephthasen* to mean "has come near."[36] The exegete will have to test such a statement and, accordingly, decide whether or not he must alter his interpretation of the Matthean text.

When in Matthew 12:29 the saying about overpowering the Strong Man now follows as an argument against the charge of being in league with demons, it has the effect of an afterthought or postscript, as the analysis has already shown. A glance at the Marcan parallel shows that Matthew follows the Marcan text almost word for word, but since the same saying also occurs in this place in another version in Luke 11:21 f., it obviously stood here in Q: from this it follows that the original context of Mark 3:26 f., which we have in Mark, has in Q been expanded by the addition of the material in Matthew 12:27 f. (= Luke 11:19 f.). Since Matthew follows Q in the sequence of these verses, it is superfluous to look for a connection in thought between Matthew 12:28 and 12:29 as though deliberately intended by Matthew. Since no application of the saying about the Strong Man is given, one must be inferred; the commentaries on Matthew offer little help on this point, so that one must turn to commentaries on Mark 3:27 (cf. Taylor and Grundmann). Again obviously following Q (cf. Luke 11:23), Matthew temporarily concludes this train of thought with the saying, "He who is not with me . . ." (12:30), which "warns against being uncommitted" (Klostermann). It is clear that this saying, which is in some way intended to refer to the necessity for following Jesus, does not originally belong to this context; what precise sense Matthew meant to give it is also unclear, since all indications are lacking. The commentaries discuss several possible explanations, but it is well to be aware that we have hardly anything here on which to base a certain interpretation.

The subject changes again and there follows the double

saying of Matthew 12:31 f., which first declares that all blasphemy is forgivable except that against the Spirit and then says that speaking against the Son of man is forgivable, but that speaking against the Holy Spirit is unforgivable. If we seek to understand this double saying in the context of Matthew's Gospel, we find that its connection with the preceding and following material is quite as obscure as the reason for the radically different valuation of rejecting the Son of man and rejecting the Holy Spirit. For it is not said that this double saying is supposed to be related to the charge of being in league with demons, and it can at most be *inferred* from the fact that the working of the Spirit in Jesus' demon exorcisms was mentioned in 12:28. Why speaking against the Son of man is described as forgivable in verse 32 can only be guessed at. Here too, of course, the exegete will take the Synoptic parallels into account before he turns to the commentaries, and he will notice first that Matthew combines the version of the saying in Mark 3:28 f. with that in Luke 12:10 (from Q); he will also notice, however, that Matthew has more strongly emphasized the *eternal* unforgivableness of speaking against the Holy Spirit. But, above all, he will notice that in Mark 3:28 f. the distinction between the Son of man and the Holy Spirit is lacking, and, further, that Mark explicitly connects this saying with the accusation that Jesus is in league with demons. This comparison thus shows clearly that Matthew has been consciously composing here and, therefore, the contrast between the eternal unforgivableness of blasphemy against the Holy Spirit and the forgivability of blasphemy against the Son of man is obviously due to him. However, if one looks to the commentaries for help in understanding this contrast, one finds that every commentator offers a different explanation, since, in fact, we have no real possibility of answering this question.[37] The interpreter of Matthew must admit, for better or for worse, that the meaning of these two verses cannot be explained with any certainty, and then it only remains necessary to ask whether the version of the saying in Mark 3:28 is perhaps more original or, at least, more intelligible.[38] Thus, here again, the exegesis of Matthew leads necessarily to the problem of the oldest tradition and its relationship to Jesus.

In Matthew there now follows (in 12:33-37) a loosely connected series of sayings whose relationship to what precedes is not immediately understandable. The discussion in Schmid's commentary shows that the saying about the tree and the fruit in verse 33 can apply equally well to Jesus (if the healings of demoniacs are not evil, then the one who performs them cannot be evil, and vice versa) and to the Pharisees (their calumny against Jesus proves that they are themselves evil; cf. verses 34 f.). On the first interpretation the *poiēsate* in verse 33 is easily understood, but the transition to verses 34 f. is awkward, since these verses *must* refer to the Pharisees; on the second interpretation the *poiēsate* is difficult, and one must understand it in a weakened sense ("suppose the tree is good . . ."[39]) which gives a unity to verses 33-35 in that they then all deal with the true nature of the Pharisees. Since it seems impossible to decide for one interpretation or the other in the context of Matthew, one will again turn to the Lucan parallel 6:43-45, which comes at the end of the Lucan Sermon on the Plain. In wording (but not altogether in the order of the words) it corresponds by and large to Matthew 12:33-35; the Matthean parallel to Luke 6:44b ("Figs are not gathered from thorns . . ."), however, is found not here, but at the end of the Sermon on the Mount (Matthew 7:16b), and Matthew 12:34a ("You brood of vipers!") has no parallel in Luke. Now it is hardly possible to give a straightforward explanation of the relationship of the three texts (Matthew 12:33-

35, its parallel in Luke 6:43-45, and Matthew 7:16-18, 20) to one another,[40] but the comparison just made leads us to suppose that the extra material in Matthew 12:34*a* was added to the tradition by Matthew (see Klostermann; and Bultmann, *History of the Synoptic Tradition,* 95[2]), and, hence, it is likely that Matthew applied verse 33 to the Pharisees. In this case, therefore, the Synoptic comparison helps us to reach a more certain interpretation of the Matthean text.

Matthew concludes the whole section in verses 36 f. with a saying about the enduring consequences of human speech; this has no Synoptic parallel and is, therefore, from Matthew's special source. Though the saying is quite general in its formulation, Matthew has probably applied it to the Pharisees for having accused Jesus of being in league with demons, and in this connection Klostermann's commentary refers to A. Jülicher,[41] who, among others, interprets *rhēma argon* as "invective," on the basis of a supposed Aramaic original. Here, however, one must proceed with proper attention to exegetical method. Since Matthew elsewhere uses *argos* only once, and then with the meaning "idle" (20:3), we have no reason to ascribe the sense "abusive" to the evangelist, especially since he probably took over this saying in the Greek language. At most, then, one could understand the meaning suggested by Klostermann as an older sense of the saying, found *before* Matthew. But since the saying is formulated in quite general terms, one will have to suppose a more general meaning for even the pre-Matthean sense of the saying, and the student can discover from Strack-Billerbeck (I, 693) that similar sayings were made by the rabbis, and, from *TDNT* (I, 452, s.v. *argos*), that *argos* in Matthew 12:36 is, in the context of verse 34, to be interpreted as synonymous with *ponēros*.[42] Whether or not this meaning is appropriate in the context of

Jesus' discourse, or whether one should perhaps refuse to attribute this saying to Jesus, or whether one should give it, hypothetically, another meaning on Jesus' lips, are questions which exegesis cannot answer, but which the exegete must not evade, if he wishes to understand the saying of Jesus in its extended meaning. Here again exegesis leads of necessity to biblical theology and, therefore, also to the historical question about the outlook of Jesus, of Paul, etc. But to embark upon these methodological researches is not the task of this introductory methodological guide for beginners.

AUTHORS' AND TRANSLATOR'S NOTES

A list of abbreviations used will be found at the end of the notes.

Bibliographical references are repeated in all places where it appeared appropriate to the author to do so—to spare the reader time-consuming search. When English translations of German works exist, they have been substituted where appropriate.

Notes that appear in brackets are by the Translator.

OTTO KAISER: *Old Testament Exegesis*

1. Cf. perhaps E. Brunner, *Revelation and Reason,* trans. O. Wyon (Philadelphia: Westminster Press, 1946), pp. 118 ff.; on the question of the necessity for and the limitations of scientific theological investigation, one may profitably consult C. H. Ratschow, *Die Bedeutung der Theologie für Kirche und Gemeinde* (Bad Salzuflen: Glauben und Leben 3, 1963).

2. Cf. Rudolf Bultmann, "Das Problem der Hermeneutik," *ZThK* 47 (1950), pp. 47 ff. = Glauben und Verstehen II (Tübingen 1952), pp. 211 ff., [and A. N. Wilder, "NT Hermeneutics Today," *Current Issues in NT Interpretation, Essays in Honor of O. A. Piper* (1962), pp. 38 ff.]

3. On the objectivity of the exegete, cf. R. Bultmann, "Ist voraussetzungslose Exegese möglich?" *Festgabe für W. Baumgartner, ThZ* 13, 6 (1957), pp. 409 ff.

4. O. F. Bollnow, "Was heisst, einen Schriftsteller besser

verstehen, als er sich selber verstanden hat?" in *Das Verstehen: Drei Aufsätze zur Theorie der Geisteswissenschaften* (Mainz, 1949), p. 25.

5. Cf. Ratschow, *op. cit.,* pp. 46 ff.

6. Cf. C. Westermann (ed.), *Essays on Old Testament Hermeneutics* (Richmond: John Knox Press, 1963); the relevant contributions in A. Weiser's *Glaube und Geschichte im Alten Testament und andere ausgewählte Schriften* (Göttingen, 1961); and O. Kaiser, "Wort des Propheten und Wort Gottes," in the *Festschrift* for A. Weiser (Göttingen, 1963), pp. 75 ff. For the difference between Protestant and Roman Catholic exegesis, cf. R. Schnackenburg, *Bile* 5, (1964), pp. 234 f.

[7. Referred to as ASV; this diverges only slightly from the English Revised Version (ERV or RV) of 1881-85. The references to these and other English versions in this paragraph have been supplied by the translator. The original refers to the following German versions: E. Kautzsch and A. Bertholet, *Die Heilige Schrift des Alten Testaments* (Tübingen, I, 1922; II, 1923[4]); E. Kautzsch, *Apokryphen und Pseudepigraphen des Alten Testaments* (Tübingen, I and II, 1900 [1921] = Darmstadt, 1962), the Zürich Bible (*Zürcher Bibel*) (Zürich, 1931); and P. Riessler, *Altjüdisches Schrifttum ausserhalb der Bibel* (Augsburg, 1928).]

[8. The Old Testament translation is by J. M. P. Smith and other scholars; the New Testament translation is by E. J. Goodspeed.]

[9. The RSV; a revision of the more woodenly literal ASV (cf. note 7).]

[10. Among these may be mentioned two Roman Catholic translations, that of the Confraternity on Christian Doctrine (Paterson, N.J., 1952) and the "Jerusalem Bible" (New York: Doubleday, 1966), and the translation made under the auspices of the Jewish Publication Society of America (Philadelphia, 1962). The New English Bible (NEB) has not yet been completed; the New Testament portion was published in 1961.]

[11. 2 vols. (London: Oxford University Press, 1913).]

12. For students who have only English the *Hebrew and*

English Lexicon of the Old Testament, by Brown, Driver, and Briggs (last reprinted 1951) is still acceptable; this is based on the *Hebräisches und Aramäisches Handwörterbuch über das Alten Testament* of W. Gesenius, which has been further revised by F. Bühl (last reprinted 1962). Since lexicography has made some progress in the meantime, one should consult, at least in the case of obscure forms and words whose meaning is in doubt, the *Lexicon in Veteris Testamenti Libros,* the Hebrew portion of which has been revised by L. Köhler and the Aramaic by W. Baumgartner (Leiden, 1958[2]). [This work gives meanings in both English and German.] Here also the more recent literature on the study of words and meanings is cited. In addition to his introductory school-grammar the student should refer to the *Hebrew Grammar* of W. Gesenius and E. Kautzsch, 2nd English edition (revised in accordance with the 28th German edition [1909]) by A. E. Cowley, reprinted 1960 (London: Oxford University Press), with its detailed indices, as well as the unfinished 29th edition, revised by G. Bergstrasser (Leipzig, 1918 f.) In the field of syntax we have a comprehensive work from the pen of C. Brockelmann (Neukirchen: Kr. Moers, 1956). Even this does not exhaust the problems connected with this subject, as may be seen from the researches of D. Michel in "Tempora und Satzstellung in den Psalmen," *AEvTh* 1 (Bonn, 1960), and O. Rössler, *ZAW* 74 (1962), pp. 125-141. The most modern relevant work which surveys this whole area is the *Hebräische Grammatik* of G. Beer in the completely revised edition of R. Meyer, which appeared in three volumes in the Sammlung Göschen between 1952 and 1960 (Berlin). For the Aramaic portions of the Old Testament the work of F. Rosenthal, *A Grammar of Biblical Aramaic* (Wiesbaden, 1961) may be recommended, in addition to the *Grammatik des Biblisch-Aramäischen* (Halle, 1927) and the *Kurzgefasste Biblische-Aramäische Grammatik* (Halle, 1929), both by H. Bauer and P. Leander.

13. *Septuaginta,* ed. A. Rahlfs, 2 vols. (Stuttgart, 1935); *Biblia Sacra iuxta Vulgatam Clementinam* (Rome, Tournais, and Paris, 1927; reprinted 1956).

14. A. v. Gall, *Der hebräische Pentateuch der Samaritaner* (Giessen, 1914-1918 = Berlin, 1963).

15. Cf. Chr. Burchard, *Bibliographie zu den Handschriften vom Toten Meer, BZAW* 76 (Berlin, 1957 [1959[2]]).

16. O. Eissfeldt, *The Old Testament: An Introduction, Including the Apocrypha and Pseudepigrapha, and also the works of similar type from Qumran* (New York: Harper, 1965); A. Weiser, *The Old Testament: Its Formation and Development* (New York: Association Press, 1961); E. Sellin and L. Rost, *Einleitung in das Alte Testament* (Heidelberg, 1959[9]); A. Lods, *Histoire de la Littérature Hébraïque et Juive* (Paris, 1950); A. Bentzen, *Introduction to the Old Testament,* 2 vols. (Copenhagen, 1958[4]); R. H. Pfeiffer, *Introduction to the Old Testament* (New York, 1948); N. G. Gottwald, *A Light to the Nations: An Introduction to the Old Testament* (New York, 1959); and, though quite short, G. W. Anderson, *A Critical Introduction to the Old Testament* (London, 1959 [reprinted 1960]).

17. Cf. P. Kahle, *The Cairo Geniza* (London: Oxford University Press, 1959[2]); F. G. Kenyon, *The Text of the Greek Bible* (London: Duckworth, 1958); F. Stummer, *Einführung in die lateinische Bibel* (Paderborn, 1928).

18. Oxford: Blackwell, 1957 (3rd German edition, 1963).

19. Philadelphia: Fortress Press, 1965.

20. Cf. Würthwein, *op. cit.,* pp. 76 ff.

21. Here the indispensable tool for scholarly work is Salomon Mandelkern's *Veteris Testamenti Concordantiae Hebraicae atque Chaldaicae,* last reprinted in Graz in 1955. When making use of this concordance it should be noted that the pronouns, the relative particle *'ašer,* the Aramaic concordance and the list of proper names, including the forms denoting God and forms of the divine name Yahweh are collected at the end of the second volume. For everyday use the student will find the *Konkordanz zum Hebräischen Alten Testament,* by G. Lisowsky (Stuttgart, 1958), to be adequate.

22. For the pertinent lexicons see below, p. 84, note 4 [in the section on NT exegesis].

23. Cf. E. Würthwein, *op. cit.,* pp. 80 f.

24. On the problem of meter, cf. the relevant sections of the introductions mentioned in note 16 above, in which further bibliography will be found. For the significance of meter for textual criticism, see M. Noth, *The Old Testament World,* pp. 321 f.

25. Information about these will also be found in the introductions mentioned in note 16; cf. also *RGG* II³, cols. 996 ff.

26. Cf. note 16, above.

27. For work on the Pentateuch and the book of Joshua the *Einleitung in den Hexateuch mit Tabellen über die Quellenscheidung* by H. Holzinger (Tübingen, 1900), if used intelligently, still gives good service. A brief survey is offered in the *Hexateuchsynopse* of O. Eissfeldt (Leipzig, 1922 = Darmstadt, 1962²). M. Noth, *Überlieferungsgeschichte des Pentateuch* (Stuttgart, 1948 [= 1960²]) and G. Hölscher, *Geschichtsschreibung in Israel, SKHVL* 50 (Lund, 1952), also contain surveys presented in tabular form. In using any of these works the student should, of course, carefully take into consideration the basic viewpoint of the author. The application of the criteria of literary criticism in the study of the Pentateuch has been most recently treated, in exemplary fashion, by M. Noth, *op. cit.,* pp. 20 ff. A brief guide to literary criticism in the study of prophetic texts is implicitly contained in G. W. Anderson's *Introduction,* pp. 98 ff.

27a. Some well-chosen examples for introducing the beginner to the problems dealt with here are to be found in K. Koch's *Was ist Formgeschichte?* (Neukirchen: Kr. Moers, 1964).

[28. Literally, "situation in life." The German phrase has been adopted as a technical term by almost all writers on the subject.]

29. *Einleitung in die Psalmen, HK,* Ergänzungsband zur II. Abtlg. (Göttingen, 1933), p. 10.

30. Cf. Gunkel-Begrich, *Einleitung in die Psalmen;* O. Eissfeldt, *Der Maschal im Alten Testament, BZAW* 24 (Giessen, 1913); A. Alt, "The Origins of Israelite Law," in *Essays in Old Testament History and Religion* (1966); cf. also H. Gese, "Beobachtungen zum Stil alttestamentlicher Rechtssätze," *ThLZ* 85 (1960), cols. 147-150; G. Hölscher, *Geschichtsschreibung in Israel* (Lund, 1952); W. Richter, *Traditionsgeschichtliche Untersuchungen zum Richterbuch, BBB* 18 (Bonn, 1963); C. Westermann, *The Praise of God in the Psalms* (Richmond: John Knox Press, 1965).

31. W. Kayser, *Das sprachliche Kunstwerk* (Bern und München, 1959), p. 329. A detailed introduction to the problems will be found here.

32. Garden City, N.Y.: Doubleday Anchor Books, 1957 (German: Sammlung Dalp 90 [Bern, 1959²]).

33. *Ibid.*, p. 11.

34. *Ibid.*, p. 19.

35. For the poetic categories, cf. for details, in addition to the introductions and the commentaries on the Psalms, H. Gunkel and J. Begrich, *Einleitung in die Psalmen, HK* (Göttingen, 1933); C. Westermann, *The Praise of God in the Psalms* (cf. note 30). Further bibliography will be found in these works.

36. Cf. H. Gunkel, *Die Propheten als Schriftsteller und Dichter, SAT* II, 2 (Göttingen, 1923²), pp. XXXIV ff.; C. Westermann, *Grundformen prophetischer Rede, BEvTh* 31 (München, 1964²).

37. Aside from the relevant details given in the introductions, reference should also be made to the description of the Israelite sagas in H. Gunkel's *The Legends of Genesis* (New York: Schocken, 1964), with introduction by W. F. Albright, and to the work of A. Jolles, *Einfache Formen* (Halle, 1930 = Tübingen, 1958²), which clarifies the concepts involved and points out the connections between genre and content. C. Westermann, "Arten der Erzählung in der Genesis," in *Forschung am Alten Testament, ThB* 24 (Munich, 1964), pp. 9-91, is also useful.

38. For the distinction between apodeictic and casuistic legal maxims cf. A. Alt, "The Origins of Israelite Law" (cf. note 30).

39. Cf. also *RGG* VI³, cols. 968 f.

40. As basic works for the study of the Psalms from the point of view of "tradition criticism" (*Traditionsgeschichte*) the following may be mentioned: S. Mowinckel, *Psalmenstudien II: Das Thronbesteigungsfest Jahwäs und der Ursprung der Eschatologie* (Kristiania, 1922 = Amsterdam, 1960) [and the same author's *The Psalms in Israel's Worship* (Oxford, 1962)]; A. Weiser, *The Psalms: a Commentary* (Philadelphia, 1962); H. J. Kraus, *Worship in Israel: a Cultic History of the Old Testament* (Oxford, 1966), and the same author's *Die Königsherrschaft Gottes im Alten Testament, BHT* 13 (Tübingen, 1951), as well as J. Jeremias, *Theophanie, WMANT* 10 (Neukirchen: Kr. Moers, 1965). For the Pentateuch and for the historiography of the Deuteronomic school and of the "Chronicler," cf. M. Noth, *Überlieferungsgeschichtliche Studien* (Halle, 1943 = Tübingen, 1957²) and, by the same author, *Überlieferungsgeschichte des Pentateuch* (Stuttgart, 1948 [= 1960²]). Both these studies continue Noth's *History of Israel* (2nd ed.; New York: Harper & Row, 1960) and elucidate the relationship between literary criticism, form criticism, and tradition criticism in actual historical study. For the legal codes comparable studies may be found in the following: A. Alt's work mentioned in note 30, above; M. Noth, *Die Gesetze im Pentateuch, SKG* 17, 2 (Halle, 1940 [= *ThB* 6, Munich, 1957, pp. 9-141]); R. Rendtorff, *Die Gesetze der Priesterschrift, FRLANT* 62 (Göttingen, 1954); K. Koch, *Die Priesterschrift von Exodus 25 bis Leviticus 16, FRLANT* 71 (Göttingen, 1959); E. Gerstenberger, *Wesen und Herkunft des sogenannten apodiktischen Rechts im Alten Testament* (Diss. Bonn, 1961; publication soon in *WMANT*). See also M. Noth's *Exodus, a Commentary,* and *Leviticus, a Commentary.* (Philadelphia: Westminster, 1962, 1965). G. von Rad has provided the first basic treatment of the form-critical problem of the Hexateuch in his *The Problem of the Hexateuch* (New York:

McGraw-Hill, 1966). A. Weiser (in his *Einleitung,* §13) and, more implicitly, W. Beyerlin (in his *Origin and History of the Oldest Sinaitic Traditions* [Oxford, 1966]) take issue with von Rad. Of the steadily increasing number of tradition-critical studies in the field of prophecy only a few will be mentioned, by way of example: E. Würthwein, "Amosstudien," *ZAW* 62 (1949/50), pp. 10-52; H. Graf Reventlow, *Das Amt des Propheten bei Amos, FRLANT* 80 (Göttingen, 1962); H. W. Wolff, *Amos' geistige Heimat, WMANT* 18 (Neukirchen: Kr. Moers, 1964); E. Würthwein, "Der Ursprung der prophetischen Gerichtsrede," *ZThK* 49 (1952), pp. 1-16; H. J. Boecker, *Redeformen des Rechtslebens im Alten Testament* (Diss. Bonn, 1959 = *WMANT* 14 [Neukirchen: Kr. Moers, 1964]); H. E. v. Waldow, *Der traditionsgeschichtliche Hintergrund der prophetischen Gerichtsreden, BZAW* 85 (Berlin, 1963); and E. Rohland, *Die Bedeutung der Erwählungstraditionen Israels für die Eschatologie der alttestamentlichen Propheten* (Diss. theol. Heidelberg, 1956). The more recent commentaries are written entirely from the point of view of tradition criticism. A history of the religion of Israel from this standpoint is to be found in G. von Rad's *Old Testament Theology,* 2 vols. (New York: Harper & Row, 1962-1965).

41. The following may be mentioned in particular: *Bibel Lexikon,* ed. H. Haag (Zürich and Cologne, 1951); *Calwer Bibellexikon,* ed. K. Gutbrod, R. Kücklich, and Th. Schlatter (Stuttgart, 1959); and above all the *Biblisch-Historische Handwörterbuch,* ed. B. Reicke and L. Rost, which is now appearing (Göttingen, I, 1962; II, 1964). [To these may be added the following reference works in English: T. K. Cheyne and J. S. Black (eds.), *Encyclopaedia Biblica,* 4 vols. (New York, 1899); James Hastings (ed.), *Dictionary of the Bible,* 5 vols. (New York, 1902); F. C. Grant and H. H. Rowley (eds.), *Hastings Dictionary of the Bible,* 1 vol. (New York: Scribners, 1963); G. A. Buttrick (ed.), *The Interpreter's Dictionary of the Bible,* 4 vols. (Nashville: Abingdon, 1962).]

42. Here should be named first of all M. Noth's *History of Israel* (2nd ed.; Harper & Row, 1960) and the *History of Israel*

by John Bright (Philadelphia, 1960), which takes a different approach to the assessment of the prehistory and early history. The comprehensive *Histoire de la Palestine depuis la conquête d'Alexandre jusqu'à l'invasion Arabe,* by F. M. Abel (Paris, 2 vols., 1952) is to be mentioned particularly for the Hellenistic and Roman periods. Of older works the following still deserve attention: R. Kittel's *Geschichte des Volkes Israel* (Gotha, I, 1923[5-6]; II, 1925[6]; III, parts 1 and 2, 1927/8); E. Sellin's *Geschichte des israelitisch-jüdischen Volkes* (Leipzig, I, 1924; II, 1932); and Th. R. Robinson and W. O. E. Oesterley's *History of Israel,* I and II (Oxford, 1932 [1957]). However, these latter works should, as a matter of principle, not be consulted without comparing them critically with a more recent presentation of the material. For the chronology of the history of Israel see *RGG* I[3], cols. 1812 ff.; III[3], cols. 942 ff. Further bibliography will be found there. A work on the history of the Near East which does justice to the most recent researches is H. Schmökel's *Geschichte des Alten Vorderasiens,* H. d. O. II, 3 (Leiden, 1957); comparable works on the history of Egypt are E. Otto's *Ägypten: Der Weg des Pharaonenreiches,* Urban Bücher, Bd. V (Stuttgart, 1953), and A. Gardiner's *Egypt of the Pharaohs* (Oxford, 1961). Both fields are dealt with in A. Scharff and A. Moortgat, *Ägypten und Vorderasien im Altertum* (München, 1950). Ancient oriental texts pertinent to the study of the history of Israel are to be found in K. Galling, *Textbuch zur Geschichte Israels* (Tübingen, 1950). Texts relevant to both religious and cultural history are included in the following collections: *Altorientalische Texte zum Alten Testament,* ed. H. Gressmann (Berlin and Leipzig, 1926[2]); *Ancient Near Eastern Texts relating to the Old Testament,* ed. J. B. Pritchard (Princeton, N.J., 1955[2]); *Documents from Old Testament Times,* ed. D. W. Thomas (London, 1958); H. Donner and W. Röllig, *Kanaanäische und aramäische Inschriften,* I-III (Wiesbaden, 1962-64). Here the work of Gressmann should, on principle, be consulted only if no translation of the text is to be found in the more recent collections. If one wishes to be sure that one has not overlooked important essays published after the appearance of the works mentioned here, one should consult, in this and all related matters, the *Internationale Zeitschriftenschau für Bibelwissenschaft und Grenzgebiete,* which, since 1950, lists the most recent publications with brief comments. For the current year one should in addition examine the reviews in the last numbers of the *Zeitschrift für die alttestamentliche Wissenschaft.*

43. An introduction to the geography of Palestine is given by M. Noth in *The Old Testament World,* pp. 1-48; basic questions of historical geography are treated in the same work in pp. 49-104. The following works on this subject may also be mentioned: D. Baly, *The Geography of the Bible* (New York, 1957); F. M. Abel, *Géographie de la Palestine* (Paris, I, 1933; II, 1938); M. du Buit, *Géographie de la Terre Sainte* (Paris, 1958); J. Simons, *The Geographical and Topographical Texts of the Old Testament* (Leiden, 1959). The work of Simons and Abel's second volume are indispensable for scientific work.

44. In addition to the Bible atlases now available on the market (*Atlas of the Bible,* by L. Grollenberg [New York: Nelson, 1956], *Westminster Historical Atlas to the Bible,* of G. E. Wright, F. V. Filson, and W. F. Albright [Philadelphia, 1956[2]], and *Oxford Bible Atlas,* ed. H. G. May [London, 1962]), the *Bibelatlas,* of H. Guthe (Leipzig, 1926[2]) is still of independent value. Since the atlases give only a selection of Arabic and Israeli place names or do not indicate them at all, it will frequently be necessary to refer to a standard map of the Survey of Palestine, Survey of Jordan, or Survey of Israel, which may now be obtained without difficulty.

45. *HAT* 1 (Tübingen, 1937).

46. 1962[4], pp. 96-164.

47. Leiden, 1963.

48. Here may also be mentioned the general descriptions of W. F. Albright, *The Archeology of Palestine* (Pelican A 199; London, 1960 [1949]); G. E. Wright, *Biblical Archeology* (Philadelphia: Westminster, 1962); K. M. Kenyon, *Archeology in the Holy Land* (London, 1960); as well as the handbook *Manuel d'archéologie biblique,* of A. G. Barrois (Paris, I, 1939;

II, 1954). The series *Studies in Biblical Archeology* (London: SCM Press, 1955 ff.) has also proved useful, although it has a wider circle of readers in view. Volume IV, by A. Montet (*Ancient Egypt and the Bible*), was adversely criticized by H. Brunner (*AfO* 20, 1963, p. 193). On the problem of the historical evaluation of archeological discoveries, the basic work is M. Noth, *Der Beitrag der Archäologie zur Geschichte Israels, SVT* 7 (Leiden, 1960), pp. 262-282.

49. Bonn, 1940.

50. Pp. 145-179.

51. New York: McGraw-Hill, 1961.

52. Cf. W. Eichrodt, *Theologie des Alten Testaments* (Stuttgart and Göttingen, I, 1963[7]; II/III, 1964[5]); the first volume has been translated as *The Theology of the Old Testament* (Philadelphia: Westminster, 1961 [from an earlier edition of the German]); G. von Rad, *Old Testament Theology* (New York: Harper & Row, 1962-1965), 2 vols.; Th. C. Vriezen, *An Outline of Old Testament Theology* (Oxford: Blackwell, 1958).

52a. J. Barr, in *The Semantics of Biblical Language* (New York: Oxford University Press, 1961), emphatically warns against confused etymological, semantic, and theological misinterpretations.

53. Cf. above, note 41.

54. Cf. above, note 52.

55. Cf. below, p. 85, note 12.

56. Pp. 278-297.

57. Sammlung Kröner, 298 (Stuttgart, 1961).

58. New York, 1960[2].

59. Baltimore, 1946[2].

60. *Ibid.*

61. Chicago, 1946.

62. *JNES* 19 (1960), pp. 117-132.

63. New York, 1949 (1948).

64. Paris, 1949.

65. *RM* (Stuttgart, 1960).

66. *HAW* III, 1, III, 1 (München, 1933).

67. Berlin, 1952.

68. *SVT* 5 (Leiden, 1957). In a measure limited by their special subjects a similar purpose is served by O. Kaiser, *Die mythische Bedeutung des Meeres in Ägypten, Ugarit, und Israel, BZAW* 78 (Berlin, 1962^2), where further bibliography is given; and W. Schmidt, *Königtum Gottes in Ugarit und Israel, BZAW* 80 (Berlin, 1961).

69. *AnOr* 35 (Rome, 1955).

70. Rome, 1949.

71. *ANET*^{2}, pp. 129-155.

72. *OS* 3 (Edinburgh, 1956).

73. *BOH* 7 (Budapest, 1959).

74. Gütersloh, 1962.

75. *HAW* III, 1, III, 3, 1 (München, 1957^2).

76. Paris, 1949.

76a. I, 8, I, 1 (Leiden and Cologne, 1964), with contributions on Egyptian, Canaanite-Ugaritic, Anatolian, and Old Testament religion, by E. Otto, O. Eissfeldt, H. Otten, and J. Hempel.

77. Heidelberg, 1925.

78. Berlin and Leipzig, 1954^3 = 1927^2.

79. Princeton, N.J., 1954.

80. Gütersloh, 1961.

81. Stuttgart, 1955 ff.

82. Tübingen.

83. Freiburg, 1961^2.

84. London: Allen and Unwin, 1938; 2nd German edition, 1956.

85. Stuttgart, 1960.

86. Since the question of phenomenology as such cannot be entered into further here, reference may be made to the systematic exposition by G. v. d. Leeuw, pp. 768 ff.

87. Cf. above, note 4.

88. Cf. B. S. Childs, "Interpretation in Faith," *Interpretation* XVIII (1964), pp. 440 ff.

WERNER GEORG KÜMMEL: *New Testament Exegesis*

1. R. Bultmann, "Das Problem der Hermeneutik," *ZThK* 47 (1950), p. 51 = R. B., *Glauben und Verstehen* II (1952 [= 1961³]), p. 216. The whole essay is well worth reading. Cf. also G. Ebeling, "Hermeneutik," *RGG* III³, p. 258, and the review of the history of the hermeneutical problem which is given in this article. [English speaking readers will find the essays in *The New Hermeneutic,* ed. James M. Robinson and John B. Cobb, Jr., instructive.]

2. The 25th edition appeared in 1963. It differs essentially from the 24th only in the addition of readings from papyri discovered in the last three years. A new edition, which is in many respects more practically designed, is in preparation. [This has now appeared; it is *The Greek New Testament,* ed. by K. Aland, M. Black, B. M. Metzger, and A. Wikgren. It presents the student with fewer variant readings, but with much fuller details about those which it does present.] The Greek-Latin edition is much to be recommended (the Latin side has the official version of the Vulgate, with the variations of the modern critical text); the Greek-German edition (with Luther's translation) should not be used for exegesis. [The author would obviously also discourage English-speaking students from using a Greek-English edition of the New Testament. The reasons for this are given at the end of section II of this essay.]

3. Suitable for students are: (*a*) the somewhat more comprehensive treatments by F. G. Kenyon and A. W. Adams, *The Text of the Greek Bible* (1958), and by B. M. Metzger, *Chapters in the History of New Testament Textual Criticism* (1963); (*b*) the shorter treatments in "Introductions" to the New Testament (cf. below, note 6); (*c*) H. Lietzmann's "Einführung in die Textgeschichte der Paulusbriefe," in his commentary on the Epistle to the Romans (*HNT* 8, 1933⁴, pp. 1 ff.) and the articles "Bibelhandschriften des NT" and "Textkritik II" in *RGG*

I³, pp. 1171 ff.; VI³, pp. 716 ff. (by G. D. Kilpatrick and H. Greeven) and "Bibelhandschriften II" and "Bibeltext II" in *LThK* II², pp. 352 ff., 372 ff. (by H. J. Vogels and J. Schmidt).

4. H. G. Liddell, R. Scott, H. S. Jones, *A Greek-English Lexicon* (1940⁹); W. Bauer, *A Greek-English Lexicon of the New Testament and Other Early Christian Literature,* trans. W. F. Arndt and F. W. Gingrich (1957). [A later (5th) German edition has appeared.] The significance of this lexicon in the history of New Testament lexicography is set forth by F. W. Gingrich in "The Contributions of Professor Walter Bauer to NT Lexicography," *NTS* 9 (1962-1963), pp. 3 ff.

5. C. F. D. Moule, *An Idiom Book of New Testament Greek* (1959²; paperback).

6. New Testament introductions by the following deserve special consideration: W. Michaelis, 1961³, with supplement; A. Wikenhauser, 1962⁵ [English trans., 1963]; P. Feine and J. Behm¹², completely revised by W. G. Kümmel (1963; rev. 1965¹⁴) [English trans., 1966], W. Marxsen (1963 [= 1964³]); cf. further: *Einfürhrung in die Bibel,* II, ed. A. Robert and A. Feuillet (1965 [the French original is *Introduction à la Bible,* II (1959)]), and D. Guthrie, *New Testament Introduction,* I (Gospels and Acts), II (Pauline Epistles), and III (Hebrews-Revelation) (1961-1965).

7. See the discussion in Feine-Behm-Kümmel, *Introduction* (cf. note 6, above), §5.

8. The three fundamental works on the form criticism of the Synoptics are: M. Dibelius, *From Tradition to Gospel,* trans. B. D. Woolf; R. Bultmann, *The History of the Synoptic Tradition,* trans. John Marsh (1963); and K. L. Schmidt, *Der Rahmen der Geschichte Jesu* (1919 [1964²]). Whoever cannot work through any of these books should at least acquaint himself with the basic concepts of form criticism, perhaps by reading the article "Evangelien, formgeschichtlich" (*RGG* II³, pp. 749 ff.; G. Bornkamm) or "Formgeschichtliche Methode" (*LThK* IV², pp. 211 ff.; R. Schnackenburg) [or "Form Criti-

cism" (*IDB* II, pp. 320 f.; K. Grobel)], or the appropriate sections of the volumes on NT Introduction.

9. A short introduction is given in the author's essay, "Das Problem des geschichtlichen Jesus in der gegenwärtigen Forschungslage," in the volume *Der historische Jesus und der kerygmatische Christus* (1960 [= 1964³], pp. 48 ff. (= W. G. K., *Heilsgeschehen und Geschichte* [1965], pp. 392 ff.). [In English, cf. J. M. Robertson, *A New Quest of the Historical Jesus* (1959).]

10. C. H. Bruder, *Tamieion . . . sive Concordantiae omnium vocum Novi Testamenti Graeci* (1913⁷) and W. F. Moulton-A. S. Geden, *A Concordance to the Greek Testament* (1953³).

11. O. Schmoller, *Handkonkordanz zum griechischen NT* (1960¹²). [English-speaking students should have no difficulty using this.] A useful tool is the index volume to the Catholic "Regensburger NT": *Deutsches Wörterbuch zum NT, nach dem griechischen Grundtext bearbeitet* von G. Richter (1962), in which passages dealing with a particular idea are given in full in German and arranged according to their subject-matter. [There is nothing quite like this in English, except perhaps Harper's *Topical Bible Dictionary*.]

12. *Theological Dictionary of the New Testament,* trans. G. W. Bromiley, 3 vols. so far; the German edition (*Theologisches Wörterbuch zum Neuen Testament,* ed. G. Kittel and G. Friedrich) is now in its 7th volume.

13. *Calwer Bibellexikon* (1959⁵); above all: *Biblisch-historisches Handwörterbuch,* ed. B. Reicke and L. Rost (vol. I, A-G, 1962, II, H-0, 1964). [In English one may consult the *Interpreter's Dictionary of the Bible,* 4 vols. (1962); Hastings' *Dictionary of the Bible* (4 vols. + extra volume; the one-volume edition of this work has recently been brought up to date, but the articles in the older, larger work are still valuable); *Encyclopaedia Biblica;* Hastings' *Dictionary of Christ and the Gospels;* Hastings' *Dictionary of the Apostolic Age;* and Hastings' *Encyclopaedia of Religion and Ethics*.]

14. H. Lietzmann, *Handbuch zum NT* (1933[4]); O. Michel, *Kritisch-exegetischer Kommentar über das NT,* begründet von H. A. W. Meyer ([1955[10]] 1963[12]); O. Kuss, *Der Römerbrief übersetzt und erklärt,* 1. Lief. (1957). [For commentaries in English the translator will refer to W. Sanday and A. C. Headlam, *The Epistle to the Romans (ICC)*; C. K. Barrett, *A Commentary of the Epistle to the Romans* (1957); F. F. Bruce, *The Epistle of Paul to the Romans* (1963); and K. H. Schelkle, *The Epistle to the Romans* (1964). Of these Sanday and Headlam and Barrett are more philologically oriented, Bruce is conservative, and Schelkle is a Roman Catholic. Sanday and Headlam's commentary is much more detailed than the others, and is the only one that makes extensive use of the Greek text.]

15. If doubts have been raised about the originality of the context in which a text has come down to us (e.g., according to widely held views, in the Corinthian and Philippian epistles), the exegete must endeavor to form his own opinion about the original context of the text and, in general, to ask whether another context can be found which has a better claim to be original. At all events the interpreter must have clearly in mind whether he intends to interpret the text as a component part of its traditional context, of some hypothetical context, or as having no discoverable original context.

16. See the names in Feine-Behm-Kümmel (cf. note 6, above), §19, 1.

17. On methodological grounds the consultation of other commentaries is avoided here, although this is helpful in many cases.

18. It should be noted that Schmoller's concordance is not simply a mechanical listing of the occurrences of all words, but that it has them sorted into groups (thus, e.g., under *eirēnē* its occurrences in the introductory passages in Paul's epistles and in the formula "the God of peace" are grouped together). For this reason one must take care not to overlook occurrences of a word that may have been listed earlier in an article and also, if circumstances warrant it, one should critically examine the

grouping to which Schmoller has assigned a particular occurrence of a word.

19. E. Haenchen, in his commentary on Acts (1965[14]), p. 108, note 6, gives an exhaustive list of such passages.

20. Blass-Debrunner's *Grammar* (§§341 and 342,2) points out that *hestēka* has present meaning.

21. If one refers to the passage cited, Psalm 5:12, in Rahlfs' edition of the Septuagint, one finds *en* in the text and *epi* in the apparatus, which shows that the two prepositions were interchangeable after *kauchasthai*. An edition of the Septuagint is as valuable for the exegesis of the Old Testament as it is for understanding the language of the New Testament.

22. Here a glance at the margin of Nestle informs us that Romans 3:23 speaks negatively of the loss of *doxa*, while Romans 8:18 likewise speaks of the expectation of *doxa* for the eschatological future.

23. Above all the article *pneuma* in *TWNT*, VI, esp. pp. 413 ff.; further references for NT theology and Pauline theology are given there. [Vol. VI of *TWNT* has not yet been translated as a whole, but this article has been translated separately as *Spirit of God*, by Eduard Schweizer (trans. A. E. Harvey, in the *Bible Key Words* series); see esp. pp. 54-87.]

24. Reference to *TDNT* (II, 214 ff.; G. Schrenk, I, 172 ff.; J. Behm) confirms these observations. The investigation of Paul's use of *en* by F. Neugebauer, *In Christus* (1961), pp. 34 ff., esp. p. 43, shows that we have here a characteristic Pauline use of *en* in the sense of an "adverbial modification." [English speaking students may consult E. Best, *One Body in Christ*, pp. 1-33, with profit.]

25. H. Strack-P. Billerbeck, *Kommentar zum Neuen Testament aus Talmud und Midrasch*, III (1926), 223 ff. This work is not a commentary in the ordinary sense, but a comprehensive collection of Jewish parallels to all ideas and customs in the New Testament which could have a Jewish origin. Good index volumes now also make it possible to find out the exact wording of rabbinical texts cited in this work only by abbrevi-

ated references. [This work, unfortunately, has not been translated, and there is no equivalent work in English.]

26. Perhaps *EKL* III, pp. 1652 f.; *RGG* VI³, pp. 1371
ff.; *CBL,* pp. 1361 f.; R. Bultmann, *Theology of the New Testament,* §33; G. Wiencke, *Paulus über Jesu Tod* (1939), pp. 69
ff. [Additional references in English are *IDB,* I, 309-313; John
Knox, *The Death of Christ.*]

27. E. Klostermann, *Handbuch zum NT,* 4 (1927²); J.
Schniewind, *Das NT Deutsch* (1937 [= 1964¹¹]); J. Schmid,
Regensburger NT (1956³); Klostermann is historically and critically oriented, Schniewind strongly theological, Schmid Catholic
and critical. For Mark: E. Lohmeyer, *Meyers Kommentar*
(1951¹¹) with supplement; V. Taylor, *The Gospel according to
St. Mark* (1952); W. Grundmann, *Theologischer Handkom-
mentar zum NT* (1959²). Lohmeyer is moderately critical, Taylor conservative, Grundmann both critical and biblicistic. For
Luke: E. Klostermann, *Handbuch zum NT,* 5 (1929²); K. H.
Rengstorf, *Das NT Deutsch* (1962⁹). Klostermann is again historically and critically oriented, Rengstorf conservative. [The
translator has added occasional references to the following commentaries in English: for Matthew, W. C. Allen (1907); A. H.
McNeile (1957); A. Plummer (n.d.); for Mark, C. B. Cranfield
(1959); S. E. Johnson (1960); for Luke, J. M. Creed (1957);
A. Plummer (1900).]

28. The best at present is the *Synopsis Quattuor Evange-
liorum,* ed. K. Aland (1964).

29. Cf. Taylor, *Mark,* pp. 237, 240 f. For the analysis of
a Synoptic text one will also always refer to R. Bultmann's *History of the Synoptic Tradition* (in our case, pp. 13 f.) and, if
the passage is treated there, M. Dibelius' *From Tradition to Gospel* (in our case, pp. 222 f.).

30. It is strongly recommended that the student impress
upon himself the agreements and disagreements in the wording
of the Synoptic Gospels by making appropriate underlining,
with different colored pencils, in a copy of a Synopsis. A useful
scheme for underlining is given by F. C. Grant in *The Growth of
the Gospels.*

31. The historical questions, whether the demon exorcism, which is lacking in Mark, formed the original introduction to the narrative, and why Matthew, contrary to his own doublet in 9:32-34 and contrary to Luke 11:14, speaks of a blind *and* dumb demoniac, are both important for critical study of the tradition, but do not contribute to the understanding of the Matthean text.

32. *TDNT* II, 1 ff.; W. Foerster. [The article on *satanas,* in *TWNT* VII, 151 ff., has not been translated; see, perhaps, the article "Satan" in *IDB*.]

33. It is the same in profane Greek, as one can see from Liddell-Scott (see note 4, above), p. 1927, under II, 2, and IV, 1.

34. This question is very difficult to decide.

35. A glance at Bultmann's *History of the Synoptic Tradition,* as recommended in note 29, will confirm this observation (p. 14).

36. Cf., e.g., E. Grässer, *Das Problem der Parusieverzögerung in den synoptischen Evangelien und in der Apostelgeschichte* (1957 [=1960²]), p. 7; contrast, e.g., W. G. Kümmel, *Promise and Fulfilment: The Eschatological Message of Jesus* (1957), pp. 99 f.

37. Klostermann leaves the question unanswered, and Schmid does not discuss the problem at all. Schniewind thinks that the saying about blasphemy against the Son of man reflects an opinion that Jesus was merely human, but this goes against Matthew's linguistic usage. [McNeile suggests that "Son of man" means simply "man" here, and refers to the Aramaic use of *bar nasha* in this sense. Allen suggests that Mark's *tois huiois tōn anthrōpōn* and Matthew's *kata tou huiou tou anthrōpou* go back to the same Aramaic phrase, and that Matthew has misunderstood it. Plummer thinks that "Son of man" here refers to Christ in his human life on earth.]

38. To be sure, if the commentaries used normally in one's exegetical work give no answer or no satisfactory answer to an individual problem, one will consult further commentaries and other literature about Jesus, Paul, etc. Whether any commen-

tary whatever is successful in explaining the sense of Matthew 12:31 f. in the context of Matthew's Gospel is, to me, very doubtful. If one supposes the originality of Mark 3:28 f., the formation of the version of the saying in Q may nevertheless be understood as an expression by the Christian community of its differing attitudes toward the human Son of man, on the one hand, and the Risen Christ, active in the Spirit, on the other. Further discussion of the antiquity and original meaning of Mark's version of the saying may be found in Bultmann's *History of the Synoptic Tradition,* pp. 403 f., and in the most recent works on the Son of man (H. E. Tödt, *The Son of Man in the Synoptic Tradition* [1965], pp. 109 ff., 282 ff.; F. Hahn, *Christologische Hoheitstitel* [1963], pp. 299 f.; A. J. B. Higgins, *Jesus and the Son of Man* [1964], pp. 127 ff.).

39. See Bauer's *Lexicon,* p. 688, under e β.

40. Well-founded theories about the history of the tradition of this text are to be found in Bultmann, *History of the Synoptic Tradition,* pp. 74, 83 f. If no extensive treatment of the analysis of such a text can be found in works on form criticism, the student should also survey other literature about Jesus and, in the case at hand, works about the parables and the ethical teaching of Jesus in particular. Here may be mentioned J. Jeremias, *The Parables of Jesus* (1963⁶); T. W. Manson, *The Teaching of Jesus* (1948); also by Manson, *The Sayings of Jesus* (1950).

41. A. Jülicher, *Die Gleichnisreden Jesu* II (1898 [= 1910²]), p. 126.

42. In addition it may be pointed out, since students would have some difficulty looking it up, that E. Stauffer, "Von jedem unnützen Wort?" in *Gott und die Götter,* a volume of essays in honor of E. Fascher (1959), pp. 94 ff., wants to interpret Matthew 12:36 as a demand for silence which comes from Qumran and not from Jesus. However, it may be argued that *argos* can mean not only "needless" but also "graceless, naughty, good for nothing," so that Matthew 12:36 f. could reasonably be understood to reflect Jesus' teaching that a disciple is answerable before God for all of his words, as well as for his actions.

(Cf. W. G. Kümmel, "Diakritik zwischen Jesus von Nazareth und dem Christusbild der Urkirche," in *Ein Leben für die Kirche,* a volume of essays in memory of J. Bauer [1960], pp. 59 f., = W. G. K., *Heilsgeschehen und Geschichte* [1965], pp. 386 f.).

LIST OF ABBREVIATIONS

The following abbreviations are frequently found in references to important journals and to series of commentaries and other studies on the Old and New Testaments:

AB	The Anchor Bible
AEvTh	*Abhandlungen zur evangelischen Theologie*
AfO	*Archiv für Orientforschung*
ANET	*Ancient Near Eastern Texts relating to the Old Testament*, ed. J. B. Pritchard (1955²)
AnOr	*Analecta Orientalia*
ATD	*Das Alte Testament Deutsch*
ATR	*Anglican Theological Review*
BBB	Bonner Biblische Beiträge
BEvTh	*Beiträge zur Evangelischen Theologie*
BHT	*Beiträge zur historischen Theologie*
Bib	*Biblica*
BiLe	Bibel und Leben
BJ	The Jerusalem Bible
BJRL	*Bulletin of the John Rylands Library*
BK	*Biblischer Kommentar, Altes Testament*
BNTC	Black's New Testament Commentaries
BOH	Bibliotheca Orientalis Hungarica
BR	*Biblical Research*
BWANT	*Beiträge zur Wissenschaft vom Alten und Neuen Testament*
BZ	*Biblische Zeitschrift*

BZAW	*Beihefte zur Zeitschrift für die alttestamentliche Wissenschaft*
CAT	*Commentaire de L'Ancien Testament*
CBL	*Calwer Bibellexikon*
CBQ	*Catholic Biblical Quarterly*
CGTC	*Cambridge Greek Testament Commentary*
CNT	*Commentaire du Nouveau Testament*
DBS	*Dictionnaire de la Bible,* Supplement
EBi	*Encyclopaedia Biblica*
EH	*Ecclesiastical History*
EKL	*Evangelisches Kirchenlexikon*
ExpT	*Expository Times*
FRLANT	*Forschungen zur Religion und Literatur des Alten und Neuen Testaments*
GCS	*Die griechischen christlichen Schriftsteller*
HAT	*Handbuch zum Alten Testament*
HAW	*Handbuch der Altertumswissenschaft*
HDAC	Hastings' *Dictionary Apostolic Church*
HDB	Hastings' *Dictionary of the Bible*
HDCG	Hastings' *Dictionary of Christ and the Gospel*
HK	*Handkommentar zum Alten Testament*
HNT	*Handbuch zum Neuen Testament*
HS	*Die Heilige Schrift des Alten Testaments,* ed. F. Feldmann and H. Herkenne (Bonn, 1933—).
HSAT	*Die Heilige Schrift des Alten Testaments,* ed. E. Kautzsch (Tübingen, 1896, 1909-1910); re-ed. A. Bertholet (Tübingen, 1922-1923).
HTR	*Harvard Theological Review*
HTS	*Harvard Theological Studies*
IB	*The Interpreter's Bible*
ICC	*International Critical Commentary*
IDB	*The Interpreter's Dictionary of the Bible*
Int	*Interpretation*
JBL	*Journal of Biblical Literature*
JNES	*Journal of Near Eastern Studies*
JTS	*Journal of Theological Studies*
KAT	*Kommentar zum Alten Testament*

LThK	*Lexikon für Theologie und Kirche*
Meyer	*Kritisches-exegetisches Kommentar über das Neuen Testament,* founded by H. A. W. Meyer
NovT	*Novum Testament*
NTA	*New Testament Abstracts*
NTD	*Das Neue Testament Deutsch*
NTS	*New Testament Studies*
NTTS	*New Testament Tools and Studies*
OS	*Old Testament Studies*
PW	Pauly-Wissowa, *Realencyklopädie der klassischen Altertumswissenschaft*
*RGG*³	*Die Religion in Geschichte und Gegenwart,* 3rd edition
RM	*Römische Mitteilungen des Deutschen Archäologischen Institutes*
SAT	*Die Schriften des Alten Testamentes in Auswahl übersetzt und erklärt*
SKG	*Schriften der Königsberger Gelehrten Gesellschaft, Königsberg*
SKHVL	*Skrifter utgivna av kungl. Humanistiska Vetenskapssamfundet i Lund*
SVT	Supplements to *Vetus Testamentum*
TDNT	*Theological Dictionary of the New Testament*
ThB	*Theologisch Bücherei. Neudrucke und Berichte aus dem 20. Jahrhundert*
ThLZ	*Theologische Literaturzeitung*
ThSt	*Theologische Studien*
ThZ	*Theologische Zeitschrift*
TWNT	*Theologisches Wörterbuch zum Neuen Testament*
VigChr	*Vigiliae Christianae*
VT	*Vetus Testamentum*
WMANT	*Wissenschaftliche Monographien zum Alten und Neuen Testament*
ZAW	*Zeitschrift für die alttestamentlichen Wissenschaft*
ZNW	*Zeitschrift für neutestamentlichen Wissenschaft*
ZThK	*Zeitschrift für Theologie und Kirche*

A